Focus on Canada

Canada's Changing Immigrant Population

By: Jane Badets
Tina W.L. Chui

Catalogue No. 96-311E

Published by Statistics Canada and Prentice Hall Canada Inc.

Statistics   Statistique
Canada   Canada

Canadä

Canadian Cataloguing in Publication Data

Badets, Jane
Chui, Tina W.L.
Canada's Changing Immigrant Population

(Focus on Canada series)
CS96-311E
Issued also in French under the title:
Évolution de la population immigrante du Canada.

1. Immigrants -- Canada -- Statistics.
2. Canada -- Emigration and immigration -- Statistics.
3. Canada -- Census, 1991.
I. Chui, Tina W.L. II. Statistics Canada. III. Title.
IV. Series: Focus on Canada (Ottawa, Ontario).

HA741.5 1991j 305.8'0971'021 C94-931060-3

Published by authority of the Minister
responsible for Statistics Canada

© Minister of Industry,
Science and Technology, 1994

ISBN 0-13-310665-9
Published by Statistics Canada and Prentice Hall Canada Inc.

Acquisitions Editor: Michael Bickerstaff, Prentice Hall Canada Inc.
Product Manager: Lorna Bailie, Statistics Canada

1 2 3 4 5   98 97 96 95 94

Printed and bound in Canada.

Distributed by: Prentice Hall Canada Inc.
                   1870 Birchmount Rd.
                   Scarborough, Ontario
                   M1P 2J7

Preface

Focus on Canada is a series of publications portraying the people of Canada. The portrait is drawn through the analysis of the data collected by the 1991 Census of Population and Housing. Each publication examines a specific issue and provides a demographic, social, cultural and economic perspective.

The authors of this series have taken special care to make their analysis informative and easy to read. They make use of descriptive graphs and data tables to more clearly illustrate the information. Often the results are compared to previous censuses, showing how Canada and Canadians have changed over time.

The publications were prepared by analysts at Statistics Canada, and reviewed by peers from within the Agency as well as experts from external organizations. I would like to extend my thanks to all the contributors for their role in producing this useful and interesting publication.

I would like to express my appreciation to the millions of Canadians who completed their questionnaires on June 4, 1991. Statistics Canada is very pleased to be able to now provide this summary of the results. I hope you enjoy reading this study -- and the others in this series.

Ivan P. Fellegi
Chief Statistician of Canada

Contents

Contents (continued)

Contents (continued)

Contents (continued)

Contents (continued)

Contents (concluded)

Highlights

- The immigrant population represented 16% (4.3 million persons) of Canada's population in 1991, almost unchanged since 1951 (15%).

- Of Canada's total 1991 immigrant population, 48% arrived in Canada before 1971, 24% between 1971 and 1980, and 28% between 1981 and 1991.

- While the majority of immigrants were born in Europe, this proportion declined from 62% in the 1986 Census to 54% in the 1991 Census. The proportion of immigrants born in Asia increased from 18% in 1986 to 25% in 1991.

- Overall, nearly one third of Canada's total population reported ethnic origins which were neither British nor French. Three-quarters of immigrants were of non-British or non-French origins, compared with one-quarter of persons born in Canada.

- Among immigrants of ethnic origins other than British or French, 38% reported single European origins. Persons of single Asian origins were the next largest group (22%), followed by single West Asian and Arab ancestry (4%) and single Black ancestry (3%).

- Immigrants were more likely to be married than persons born in Canada. Of those aged 15 and over, 66% of immigrants were married compared with 52% of the Canadian-born.

- While the labour force participation rate for all immigrants (65.2%) was lower than for persons born in Canada (68.7%), it varied by age groups. The participation rate for immigrants aged 25 to 44 (86.1%) was slightly lower than for the Canadian-born (86.9%). However, among persons 45 to 64 years of age, the participation rate for immigrants was higher (72.3%) than for the Canadian-born (67.5%).

- In 1991, a higher proportion of immigrants (14%) had university degrees than the Canadian-born (11%). At the same time, a larger proportion of immigrants (19%) than the Canadian-born (13%) also reported less than Grade 9 education.

- Regardless of age, recent immigrants who came to Canada between 1981 and 1991 tended to have higher levels of education than immigrants who arrived before 1981. In 1991, 17% of recent immigrants aged 15 and over held a university degree compared with 9% of those who came before 1961.

Introduction

Throughout Canada's history immigrants have made up an important component of the population. Successive waves of immigrants have increased the population of Canada and changed its ethnic composition. They have provided labour, capital and creativity, thereby contributing to the social and economic development of the country.

Canada's earliest immigrants were from France, Great Britain and Ireland. They were followed by Western and Eastern Europeans, as well as immigrants from Scandinavia and the United States. In the 1950s, immigrants increasingly came from Southern Europe. During the 1960s, Canada's immigration laws were altered to encourage the immigration of persons from all parts of the world. Since then, immigrants to Canada are increasingly from Asia and the Middle East, Africa, the Caribbean, and Central and South America.

The number of immigrants entering Canada and their characteristics are partly determined by government policies controlling admissions, and partly by the attractiveness of Canada for immigration, as well as the socio-economic and political climate in the sending countries. Since the late 1970s Canada's immigration policy has been guided by essentially three broad objectives: to reunite families, to provide safe haven for refugees, and to foster economic development by selecting business immigrants and skilled workers.[1] These objectives are reflected in the three classes (family, refugee and independent) under which persons are admitted into Canada as landed immigrants. Since 1967, certain independent applicants have been assessed by a point system, under which points are allotted for such factors as education and training, occupational skills, demand for the

---

[1] Employment and Immigration Canada, ***Annual Report to Parliament***, October 1990, p. 7.

applicant's occupation in Canada, the existence of pre-arranged employment, and personal factors such as age and knowledge of English or French.[2]

Using data from the 1991 Census, this study examines the changing profile of Canada's immigrants, with emphasis on the shift in the sources of recent immigrants. Chapter One examines changes in the composition and size of the immigrant population, and variations in where immigrants have settled over time. The impact of changing immigration patterns on Canada's ethnic and linguistic diversity is explored in the second chapter. Chapter Three highlights the demographic characteristics of the immigrant population, while Chapter Four examines their educational profile. The next two chapters highlight immigrants in the labour force. The study concludes with a discussion of non-permanent residents, who were enumerated for the first time in the 1991 Census.

Definitions

Immigrant population: refers to persons who are, or have been, landed immigrants in Canada. A landed immigrant is a person who is not a Canadian citizen by birth, but who has been granted the right to live in Canada permanently by immigration authorities. Some immigrants have resided in Canada for a number of years, while others are recent arrivals. Most immigrants have become Canadian citizens. Also included in the immigrant population are persons born in Canada who were not considered Canadian citizens at birth but who later obtained landed immigrant status.

Canadian-born population: refers to people who are Canadian citizens by birth. Although most were born in Canada, a small number were born outside Canada to Canadian parents.

Non-permanent residents: refers to people who at the time of the Census, held student or employment authorizations, Minister's permits or who were refugee claimants.

---

[2] Those entering in the family class made up 38% of all landed immigrants admitted between 1980 and 1991; 18% entered as refugees. The independent class is divided into business immigrants (including the self-employed, investors and entrepreneurs), assisted relatives and other independents. Only the latter two groups are assessed according to the point system, with varying criteria for each category. Assisted relatives made up 10% of landed immigrants entering between 1980 and 1991, 7% entered as business immigrants, 25% were other independents. Another 2% came as retirees (Data Source: Immigration Statistics, Annual, Employment and Immigration Canada). The 1991 Census did not collect information on the class under which landed immigrants are admitted, so this dimension cannot be incorporated in the analysis.

Chapter

1

The Changing Composition of Canada's Immigrant Population

Immigrants have represented a relatively stable proportion of Canada's population – about 16% – for several decades. They are not, however, evenly dispersed across the country. Almost all immigrants live in just four provinces (Ontario, British Columbia, Quebec and Alberta), with most in large urban centres. In recent years, there has been a substantial change in the countries from which immigrants have come. An increasing proportion is from non-European countries, with those from Asia and the Middle East accounting for the largest share of recent arrivals.

Over Four Million Immigrants

According to the Census, 4.3 million immigrants were living in Canada in 1991, representing 16.1% of the total population. Between 1986 and 1991, the size of Canada's immigrant population increased by 11%. In contrast, from 1981 to 1986, the number of immigrants grew by only 2%.

The overall size of the immigrant population reflects changes in annual target levels set by the federal government. As shown by **Chart 1.1**, the annual intake of immigrants since the beginning of this century has fluctuated considerably. Between 1911 and 1920, 1.7 million immigrants entered Canada, the largest wave of immigration in this century. The lowest number of immigrants came during the Depression years, with about 159,000 immigrants entering between 1931 and 1940.

In the past decade, the total number of immigrants admitted into the country fell from 129,000 in 1981 to 84,000 in 1985. Since 1986, however, annual levels have risen, reaching almost 231,000 in 1991. This was the highest annual number of immigrants entering Canada in 35 years.

Chart 1.1
Annual Levels of Immigration, 1901-1991

Landed immigrants (000's)

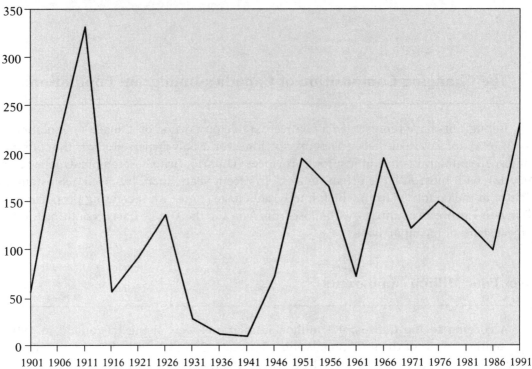

Source: *Employment and Immigration Canada*, Catalogue No. MP22-1/1991

Population Share Remains Stable

In contrast to fluctuating annual immigration levels, the proportion of immigrants in Canada's total population has been remarkably stable over the years. Since the 1951 Census, immigrants have accounted for around 16% of the total population. Earlier in the century, however, immigrants were a much larger proportion of the population, reflecting higher immigration levels. Census data show that between 1901 and 1911, the immigrant share jumped from 13% to 22%, where it remained until 1931. By 1941, the proportion of immigrants had dropped to 17% and then to 15% in 1951.

When They Arrived

Nearly half of Canada's immigrant population has lived here for more than 20 years. The proportion of immigrants is split almost evenly between those who arrived before the 1970s and those who arrived after. At the time of the 1991 Census, 48% of immigrants had arrived before 1971, while 24% had come between 1971 and 1980 and 28% between 1981 and 1991.

Where They Live

Over the years immigrants have tended to settle in certain regions of the country, with Ontario attracting the largest share in recent years. The 1991 Census showed that 94% of immigrants lived in just four provinces: Ontario, British Columbia, Quebec and Alberta. In contrast, 81% of the Canadian-born population lived in these provinces. Over half of all immigrants (55%) resided in Ontario.

Immigrants represented almost one-quarter of the provincial populations of Ontario and British Columbia in 1991, as shown in **Chart 1.2**. They also accounted for 15% of Alberta residents, 13% of Manitoba residents and 11% of those in the Yukon Territory. Immigrants made up less than 10% of the populations of the other provinces and territories.

Chart 1.2
Immigrants as a Percentage of Provincial and Territorial Populations, 1991

Percentage of immigrants

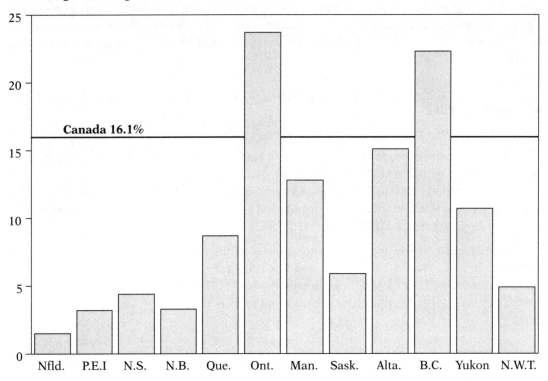

Source: Statistics Canada, *Immigration and Citizenship*. 1991 Census of Canada,
Catalogue No. 93-316.

In the early part of the century, immigrants were more likely to settle in Western Canada than in Ontario, in response to Canadian government efforts to develop that part of the country. Because of this influx into a relatively unpopulated area, immigrants accounted for much higher proportions of Western provincial populations during these early years **(Chart 1.3)**. In 1911, for example, immigrants were 57% of the populations of both British Columbia and Alberta, 50% of Saskatchewan's and 41% of Manitoba's. In contrast, 20% of Ontario's residents were immigrants in 1911. Since then, the proportion of immigrants in the Western provinces has declined steadily, whereas the proportion of immigrants in Ontario has been relatively stable, ranging from 19% to 24% of the provincial population.

The proportion of immigrants in Quebec and the Atlantic provinces has been relatively stable over time, but considerably lower than in Ontario and the Western provinces. In Quebec, for example, immigrants throughout this century have accounted for less than 10% of the provincial population. The lowest proportion was recorded in the 1901 Census, when 5.4% of Quebec's population was immigrant, while the highest proportions were recorded in the 1931 and 1991 Censuses, at 8.8% and 8.7% respectively.

Chart 1.3
Immigrants as a Percentage of Total Population, for Selected Provinces, 1901-1991

Percentage of immigrants

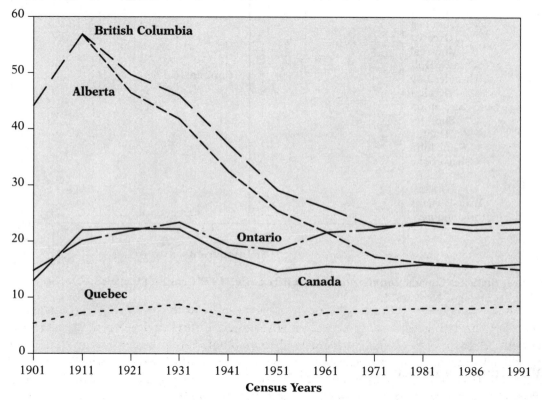

Census Years

Sources: Statistics Canada, *Population: Birthplace.* 1971 Census of Canada, Catalogue No. 92-727;
Statistics Canada, *Ethnicity, Immigration and Citizenship*. 1986 Census of Canada, Catalogue No. 93-109;
Statistics Canada, *Immigration and Citizenship*. 1991 Census of Canada, Catalogue No. 93-316.

Chart 1.4
Immigrants as a Percentage of Census Metropolitan Areas, 1991

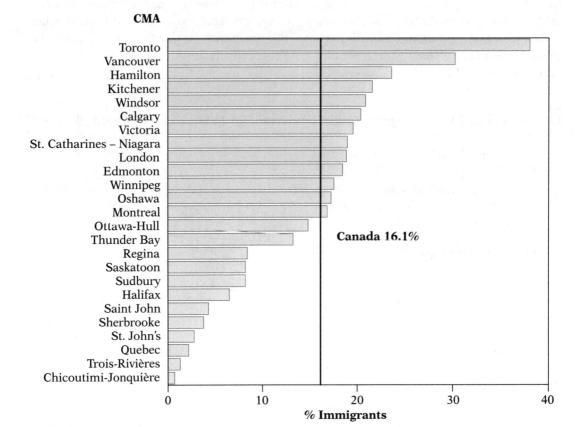

Source: Statistics Canada, *Immigration and Citizenship*. 1991 Census of Canada,
Catalogue No. 93-316.

Most Immigrants Settle in Urban Areas

Immigrants are more likely than the Canadian-born population to live in large urban areas. In 1991, more than one-half of Canada's immigrants (57%) lived in the census metropolitan areas (CMAs) of Toronto, Montreal and Vancouver. In contrast, just over one-quarter of the Canadian-born population lived in these CMAs **(see Chart 1.4)**.

Toronto had the largest immigrant population of any metropolitan area in 1991. About 1.5 million immigrants lived in the Toronto CMA, accounting for 38% of its population. Immigrants represented 30% of Vancouver's and 17% of Montreal's populations.

Other metropolitan areas in southern Ontario and the Western provinces have also attracted large numbers of immigrants. In Ontario, immigrants comprised 24% of Hamilton's population and about 20% of the populations of Kitchener (22%), Windsor (21%), London (19%) and St. Catharines-Niagara (19%). In Western Canada, Calgary and Victoria had the highest proportions of immigrants after Vancouver, with 20% each. Immigrants generally made up smaller proportions of the populations of major urban areas in Quebec and the Atlantic provinces. East of Montreal, only Halifax (at 7%) had an immigrant population greater than 5%.

The attraction of major urban centres for immigrants was most pronounced in Quebec: 88% of the province's immigrants lived in Montreal, compared with just 45% of the total provincial population. In British Columbia, 66% of the immigrant population resided in Vancouver, compared with 49% of the total population. A similar pattern occurred in Ontario, with 62% of that province's immigrant population living in the Toronto CMA, compared with 39% of all provincial residents.

Recent Arrivals Especially Attracted to CMAs

Recent immigrants were even more likely to reside in one of Canada's three largest metropolitan areas than were immigrants who have lived in Canada for some time. In 1991, two-thirds (66%) of those who came to Canada between 1981 and 1991 were living in Toronto, Montreal or Vancouver. In contrast, 43% of immigrants who arrived before 1961 resided in these urban areas. Toronto attracted the largest share of recent immigrants at 39%, and a further 14% had settled in Montreal and 13% in Vancouver.

Recent arrivals from Asia and the Middle East – the largest number of recent immigrants – were even more likely to settle in these metropolitan areas. At the time of the 1991 Census, nearly three-quarters (73%) of recent immigrants from Asia and the Middle East lived in either Toronto, Montreal or Vancouver. In fact, these immigrants accounted for 70% of all recent arrivals residing in Vancouver, 50% of those in Toronto and 44% of those in Montreal in 1991.

The Majority of Immigrants Were Born in Europe ...

Europeans still made up the largest share of the total number of immigrants living in Canada at the time of the 1991 Census, accounting for 54% of all immigrants. This proportion declined from 62% in the 1986 Census and 67% in the 1981 Census. Conversely, the percentage of the immigrant population born in Asia and the Middle East increased to 25% in 1991, from 18% in 1986 and 14% in 1981. The remainder of the total 1991 immigrant population were born in the United States (6%), the Caribbean (5%), Central and South America (5%), Africa (4%) and Oceania – Australia, New Zealand and the Pacific Islands (1%).

Chart 1.5
Immigrants by Place of Birth and Period of Immigration, Canada, 1991

Percentage

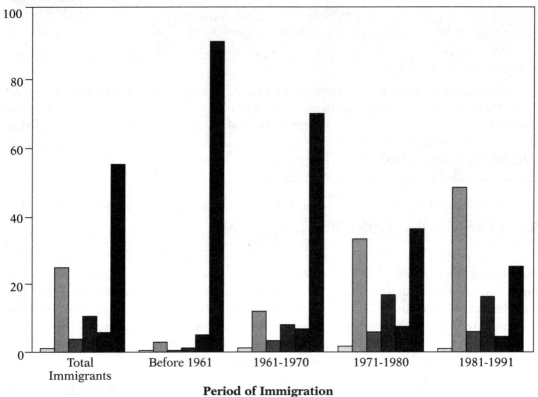

Period of Immigration

☐ Oceania & Other
▨ Asia & the Middle East
▨ Africa
■ Caribbean, South & Central America
■ U.S.A.
■ Europe

Source: Statistics Canada, *Immigration and Citizenship*. 1991 Census of Canada,
Catalogue No. 93-316.

... But the Picture is Changing

As shown in **Chart 1.5,** the proportion of European-born persons immigrating to Canada has declined steadily in recent years. Ninety percent of immigrants who arrived in Canada before 1961 were born in Europe. This proportion fell to 69% for those who arrived between 1961 and 1970; to 36% for those who immigrated between 1971 and 1980; and to one-quarter for those who arrived between 1981 and 1991.

At the same time, the proportion of immigrants born in Asia and other non-European areas has increased. People born in Asia and the Middle East made up almost one-half (48%) of immigrants who came to Canada between 1981 and 1991, but only 3% of those who came before 1961. The European-born made up the second largest group among recent immigrants (25%), with those from Eastern Europe, particularly from Poland, comprising the largest proportion of this group. An additional 10% of recent arrivals were born in Central and South America, 6% in the Caribbean, 6% in Africa, 4% in the United States and 1% in Oceania.

Top 10 Countries of Birth

Based on 1991 Census data, Asian and Middle Eastern countries accounted for six of the ten most frequently reported countries of birth for immigrants who came to Canada between 1981 and 1991. Hong Kong was at the top of the list, with 96,500 of the 1.24 million recent immigrants. Poland ranked second and the People's Republic of China, third. Among the total immigrant population, however, the countries of birth reported most often were mainly European, with the United Kingdom and Italy being the two major source countries. However, India, China and Hong Kong were also among the top ten for all immigrants. India ranked sixth, while China and Hong Kong were eighth and ninth.

Table 1.1
Top 10 Countries of Birth for All Immigrants and Recent Immigrants (1), Canada, 1991

| | All immigrants | | | Recent immigrants (1) | |
	Number	%		Number	%
Total	**4,342,890**	**100.0**	**Total**	**1,238,455**	**100.0**
1. United Kingdom	717,745	16.5	1. Hong Kong	96,540	7.8
2. Italy	351,620	8.1	2. Poland	77,455	6.3
3. United States	249,080	5.7	3. People's Republic of China	75,840	6.1
4. Poland	184,695	4.3	4. India	73,105	5.9
5. Germany	180,525	4.2	5. United Kingdom	71,365	5.8
6. India	173,670	4.0	6. Viet Nam	69,520	5.6
7. Portugal	161,180	3.7	7. Philippines	64,290	5.2
8. People's Republic of China	157,405	3.6	8. United States	55,415	4.5
9. Hong Kong	152,455	3.5	9. Portugal	35,440	2.9
10. Netherlands	129,615	3.0	10. Lebanon	34,065	2.8

(1) Immigrants who came to Canada between 1981 and 1991.

Source: 1991 Census of Canada, unpublished data.

Provincial Variations by Place of Birth

The settlement patterns of immigrants by source area varied across the country. In the Atlantic provinces, the immigrant population was largely made up of persons born in the United States (28%), the United Kingdom (31%) and other European countries (22%). Even among the recent immigrants settling in this region, the United States and the United Kingdom were the major sources, accounting for 27% and 16%, respectively. Those born in Asia and the Middle East, however, accounted for an increasing share of recent arrivals to this area: nearly one-quarter (23%) of immigrants who came between 1981 and 1991.

Compared with Canada's total immigrant population, immigrants in Quebec had higher proportions of persons born in the Caribbean, Central and South America, the Middle East and Africa. This reflects higher levels of immigration to Quebec from such places as Haiti and francophone Africa. In fact, among recent immigrants to Quebec, the percentage of African and Caribbean immigrants was nearly twice the national average. Still, in 1991, persons from Asia and the Middle East made up the largest proportion of recent arrivals in the province, accounting for 42% of immigrants who came between 1981 and 1991. These trends are reflected in the most frequent source countries for recent immigrants in Quebec. Lebanon was at the top of the list, followed by Haiti and Viet Nam. In contrast, Italy, France and Haiti were the main countries of birth for the total immigrant population in Quebec.

Because Ontario is home to over half of all immigrants in Canada, it is not surprising that its immigrant population was similar in composition to the national total. Ontario, however, had slightly higher proportions of European, Central and South American immigrants, but lower levels of Asian immigrants. Recent arrivals to Ontario reflect the national shift to non-European immigration. Among those who came between 1981 and 1991 and had settled in Ontario, almost three-quarters were from non-European countries, with the largest proportion (45%) from Asia and the Middle East. Hong Kong was the most frequent country of birth for Ontario's recent immigrants, followed by Poland, the United Kingdom, India and China. These five countries together accounted for one-third of recent immigrants in Ontario.

Just over half of all immigrants in the three Prairie provinces were born in Europe. A further 27% were from Asia and the Middle East, and 8% were from the United States. Saskatchewan had the highest proportions of immigrants from the United States (15%) and Europe (59%). Of the recent arrivals settling in the Prairies, about one-half were Asian-born, while one-quarter were from Europe. As well, the Prairies continue to attract immigrants from the United States. For example, 13% of recent arrivals in Saskatchewan and 5% in Manitoba and 6% in Alberta were American-born, compared with 4% in Ontario and 3% in Quebec.

The attraction of British Columbia for Asian-born immigrants is reflected in the composition of this province's immigrant population. One-third of all immigrants in this province were from Asia and the Middle East, compared with one-quarter at the national level. In fact, Asian-born immigrants made up 64% of recent arrivals to British Columbia. The most common countries of birth for recent immigrants in British Columbia were Hong Kong, the People's Republic of China and India. These three countries made up 38% of all recent immigrants in this province. As well, more immigrants from Oceania have settled in British Columbia than elsewhere in Canada; the proportion of recent arrivals from Oceania was 3% in British Columbia – three times the national average. As in other provinces, the proportion of European-born immigrants in British Columbia has declined from 87% of those who came before 1961 to 19% of those who came within the last decade.

The changes in the sources of immigrants since the 1960s have in turn altered the ethnic composition of Canada as these new immigrants make Canada their home and begin to raise families. The second chapter of this report looks at the role of immigration in creating a culturally diverse Canada.

Table 1.2
Percentage Distribution of All Immigrants and Recent Immigrants (1) by Place of Birth, 1991

	Newfoundland		Prince Edward Island		Nova Scotia		New Brunswick		Quebec		Ontario	
	All immi-grants	Recent immi-grants	All immi-grants	Recent immi-grants	All immi-grants	Recent immi-grants	All immi-grants	Recent immi-grants	All immi-grants	Recent immi-grants	All immi-grants	Recent immi-grants
Total	100.0	100.0	100.0	100.0	100.0	100.0	100.0	100.0	100.0	100.0	100.0	100.0
United States	21.9	14.7	32.6	28.6	24.3	27.5	35.0	31.6	4.7	3.3	4.1	3.6
Central & South America	1.6	1.6	2.4	9.1	2.0	6.3	1.4	4.0	6.5	13.2	5.5	10.4
Caribbean & Bermuda	1.9	3.5	0.7	0.0	2.1	2.3	1.1	1.2	9.6	11.9	6.5	7.3
Europe	53.4	42.0	53.9	36.0	54.2	32.2	50.5	39.6	48.6	20.3	57.9	27.6
Africa	3.7	7.2	1.0	4.6	2.3	3.7	2.3	5.7	7.8	9.5	3.3	6.0
Asia & the Middle East	15.6	29.1	7.7	17.7	13.2	25.7	8.2	16.1	22.3	41.5	22.1	44.7
Oceania & Other	2.0	1.9	1.6	4.0	2.0	2.3	1.6	1.9	0.4	0.3	0.5	0.5

	Manitoba		Saskatchewan		Alberta		British Columbia		Yukon Territory		Northwest Territories	
	All immi-grants	Recent immi-grants	All immi-grants	Recent immi-grants	All immi-grants	Recent immi-grants	All immi-grants	Recent immi-grants	All immi-grants	Recent immi-grants	All immi-grants	Recent immi-grants
Total	100.0	100.0	100.0	100.0	100.0	100.0	100.0	100.0	100.0	100.0	100.0	100.0
United States	6.1	5.3	15.0	12.5	7.8	5.6	7.5	5.5	24.5	31.5	11.1	5.8
Central & South America	8.1	13.5	3.4	7.8	4.5	8.4	2.5	4.6	1.3	3.7	2.3	3.2
Caribbean & Bermuda	3.1	2.9	1.4	1.7	2.2	2.3	0.9	0.7	2.0	5.6	3.6	4.5
Europe	54.7	23.6	58.7	25.1	50.7	25.0	49.5	18.8	60.0	38.0	56.3	37.2
Africa	1.9	3.7	2.8	8.5	4.2	5.4	2.7	2.9	1.3	2.8	3.9	7.1
Asia & the Middle East	25.6	50.7	17.9	43.2	28.9	51.3	33.8	64.1	5.7	15.7	20.7	39.1
Oceania & Other	0.5	0.3	0.8	1.1	1.7	2.0	3.0	3.3	5.1	2.8	2.3	3.2

(1) Immigrants who came between 1981 and 1991
Source: 1991 Census of Canada, unpublished data.

Statistics Canada – Catalogue No. 96-311E
Canada's Changing Immigrant Population

Chapter

2

Immigration and Ethno-cultural Diversity

Immigration has played a major role in creating a culturally diverse Canada. Since the 1960s, changes in the sources of immigrants from European to non-European countries have altered Canada's ethnic and linguistic composition. According to the 1991 Census, an increasing proportion of the population reported ethnic backgrounds other than British or French, and languages other than English or French. Moreover, the ethnic make-up of Canada varied considerably across the country – in large measure reflecting where different waves of immigrants have settled over time.

Greater Diversity in the Canadian Mosaic

Although people of British and French backgrounds were still the largest ethnic groups in Canada, neither group accounted for a majority of the population. In 1991, 28% of the population (7.6 million) were of British-only origins,[1] while 23% (6.2 million) were of French-only origins.[2] Another 4% of the population reported a combination of British and French ethnic backgrounds, while 14% reported some combination of British and/or French and other origins.

An increasing proportion of the population in 1991 reported origins other than British or French. Nearly one-third of the population (31%), as compared with one-quarter in 1986, reported an ethnic background that did not include British or French. This increase in 1991 was in part due to the growing number of recent immigrants with ethnic origins other than British or French, and to the higher proportion of the population reporting Canadian or Aboriginal origins in the 1991 Census.[3]

[1] British only origins include the single responses of English, Irish, Scottish, Welsh, other British and the multiple British only responses – that is, a combination of English, Irish, Scottish, Welsh or other British.

[2] French only origins include the single responses of French, Acadian, Québécois and the French only multiple responses – that is, a combination of French, Acadian or Québécois.

[3] Increases in Aboriginal and Canadian origins were likely the result of social and personal considerations. Public attention on Aboriginal issues in the year leading up to the Census may have contributed to increased reporting of Aboriginal origins; similarly, media publicity may have contributed to a substantial increase in the number of persons reporting Canadian origin.

Those reporting European origins comprised the largest proportion of persons having neither British nor French origins. In 1991, those reporting a European single ethnic origin made up 15% of the total population – a proportion virtually unchanged since 1986. As a result of increased immigration from non-European countries in the 1970s and 1980s, there were more people reporting non-European origins. Persons reporting Asian origins[4] represented 5.1% of the population in 1991, an increase from 3.5% in 1986. The largest Asian single response groups in 1991 were Chinese (2.2% of the total population) and East Indian (1.2%). In addition, more people reported Caribbean, Latin/Central/South American and Black single origins in 1991.

Chart 2.1a
Percentage Distribution of Population
by Ethnic Origin, Canada, 1991

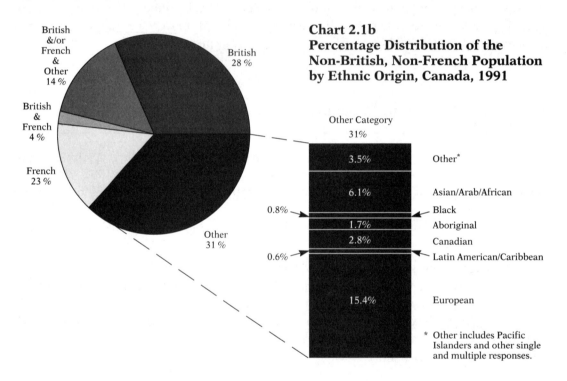

Chart 2.1b
Percentage Distribution of the
Non-British, Non-French Population
by Ethnic Origin, Canada, 1991

Source: Statistics Canada, *Ethnic Origin*. 1991 Census of Canada, Catalogue No. 93-315.

---

4   Asian origins includes South Asian, East and South East Asian single responses.

Differing Ethnic Response Patterns

In 1991, nearly eight million people, or 29% of the total population, reported more than one ethnic origin, indicating they were probably of mixed ethnic ancestry. However, the immigrant and Canadian-born population differed in their ethnic origin response patterns. Almost one-quarter of the Canadian-born population reported more than one ethnic origin, compared with one-tenth of immigrants.

The Canadian-born were also more likely to report British or French origins than were immigrants **(Table 2.1)**. For example, 99% of people reporting French-only ethnic origins, 89% reporting British-only, 98% reporting British and French, and 95% reporting British and/or French and other origins were born in Canada. In contrast, 39% of people reporting origins other than British or French were immigrants, while 59% were Canadian-born.

Table 2.1
Immigrants and the Canadian-born by Ethnic Origin, Canada, 1991

	Total population*	Canadian-born	Immigrant
Total population	**26,994,045** **100.0%**	**22,427,745** **83.1%**	**4,342,890** **16.1%**
British (1)	7,595,170 100.0%	6,772,790 89.2%	805,790 10.6%
French (2)	6,158,665 100.0%	6,081,330 98.7%	73,365 1.2%
British & French	1,071,880 100.0%	1,048,700 97.8%	22,240 2.1%
British &/or French & Other	3,832,165 100.0%	3,645,585 95.1%	177,990 4.6%
Other Origins (3)	8,336,155 100.0%	4,879,340 58.5%	3,263,505 39.1%

* Total population includes non-permanent residents.
(1) Includes British single responses and the British only multiple.
(2) Includes French single responses and the French only multiple.
(3) Includes other single responses and other multiple responses.

Source: 1991 Census of Canada, unpublished data.

The Ethnic Profile of Canada's Immigrants

In 1991, three-quarters of all immigrants reported an ethnic background that did not include British or French origins, compared with about one-quarter of people born in Canada. Europeans comprised the largest proportion (38%) of immigrants of non-British, non-French origins. Those reporting a single Asian origin represented 22% of all immigrants, followed by 4% who were of single West Asian and Arab ancestry. People of Black ancestry accounted for 3%, single Caribbean 1.5% and Latin American 1.4% of the immigrant population.

Table 2.2
Population by Ethnic Origin, Showing Immigrant Status, Canada, 1991

	Total population*	Canadian-born	All immigrants	Period of immigration	
				Before 1961	Recent immigrants (1)
	%	%	%	%	%
Total	100.0	100.0	100.0	100.0	100.0
British (2)	28.1	30.2	18.6	28.3	7.5
French (3)	22.8	27.1	1.7	1.7	1.2
British & French	4.0	4.7	0.5	0.6	0.3
British &/or French & Other	14.2	16.3	4.1	2.8	3.4
Total Other	30.9	21.8	75.1	66.6	87.6
Canadian	2.8	3.3	0.4	0.5	0.2
Aboriginal	1.7	2.1	0.1	0.0	0.1
European	15.4	11.0	37.8	60.2	21.5
Asian, Arab & African	6.1	1.7	26.4	2.3	50.7
Arab & West Asian	0.8	0.2	3.6	0.3	8.1
South Asian	1.6	0.5	6.6	0.2	10.7
East & Southeast Asian	3.6	1.0	15.7	1.7	30.8
African	0.1	0.0	0.4	0.0	1.1
Pacific Islanders	0.0	0.0	0.1	0.0	0.1
Latin American	0.3	0.1	1.4	0.0	3.4
Caribbean	0.3	0.1	1.5	0.1	2.2
Black	0.8	0.4	2.9	0.2	4.0
Other Single & Multiple Origins	3.4	3.1	4.5	3.2	5.3

* Total population includes non-permanent residents.
(1) Immigrants who came to Canada between 1981 and 1991.
(2) Includes British single responses and the British only multiple.
(3) Includes French single responses and the French only multiple.

Source: 1991 Census of Canada, unpublished data.

Among recent immigrants, there was an even higher proportion of those with origins other than British or French. At the time of the 1991 Census, 88% of immigrants who came to Canada between 1981 and 1991 were of non-British, non-French ethnic origins. This compares with 67% of immigrants who came to Canada before 1961. Asians represented the largest group among recent arrivals (42%), followed by those of single European ancestry (22%). In contrast, just 2% of immigrants who came before 1961 reported a single Asian origin, while 60% were of European heritage.

Another 8% of recent immigrants reported West Asian and Arab single origins, compared with 0.3% of immigrants who came before 1961. Likewise, 0.1% of immigrants who came before 1961 reported single Caribbean or Latin American ancestry. This figure rose to almost 6% of recent arrivals. The proportion of immigrants reporting single Black origins also increased from less than 1% of those who came before 1961 to 4% of those who came between 1981 and 1991.

Top 10 Ethnic Groups

The ethnic diversity of the immigrant population is also reflected in the top single-ethnic response groups for this population. After British, the most frequently reported origins for all immigrants were Chinese, Italian, German, East Indian and Portuguese. Among immigrants who came between 1981 and 1991, Chinese, East Indian, British, Polish and Filipino were the top single-ethnic responses. In contrast, for the Canadian-born population, the most frequent single-ethnic responses were French, British, Canadian, German, Aboriginal and Italian.

Table 2.3
Most Frequent Ethnic Origins for the Canadian-born, All Immigrants and Recent Immigrants (1), Canada, 1991

Canadian-born	Number	%	All immigrants	Number	%	Recent immigrants	Number	%
Total	22,427,745	100.0	Total	4,342,885	100.0	Total	1,238,450	100.0
Total single responses	15,150,170	67.6	Total single responses	3,852,480	88.7	Total single responses	1,116,170	90.1
Top 10 single responses			Top 10 single responses			Top 10 single responses		
1. French (2)	6,069,345	27.1	1. British (3)	702,885	16.2	1. Chinese	236,810	19.1
2. British (3)	4,893,865	21.8	2. Chinese	425,800	9.8	2. East Indian, n.i.e.	96,495	7.8
3. Canadian	745,635	3.3	3. Italian	359,070	8.3	3. British (3)	80,155	6.5
4. German	674,235	3.0	4. German	233,660	5.4	4. Polish	75,120	6.1
5. Aboriginal (4)	467,310	2.1	5. East Indian, n.i.e.	226,305	5.2	5. Filipino	58,950	4.8
6. Italian	385,075	1.7	6. Portuguese	168,935	3.9	6. Black (5)	49,675	4.0
7. Ukrainian	355,635	1.6	7. Polish	146,110	3.4	7. Vietnamese	46,085	3.7
8. Dutch(Netherlands)	221,435	1.0	8. Dutch(Netherlands)	135,440	3.1	8. Portuguese	37,945	3.1
9. Jewish	163,390	0.7	9. Black (5)	125,750	2.9	9. Spanish	32,350	2.6
10. Chinese	132,850	0.6	10. Filipino	112,520	2.6	10. Lebanese	30,120	2.4
Total multiple responses	7,277,570	32.4	Total multiple responses	490,410	11.3	Total multiple responses	122,280	9.9
British Only (6)	1,878,920	8.4	British Only (6)	102,905	2.4	British Only (6)	12,385	1.0
French Only (7)	11,980	0.1	French Only (7)	80	-	French Only (7)	--	--
British & French	1,048,700	4.7	British & French	22,240	0.5	British & French	3,635	0.3
British &/or French & Other	3,645,585	16.3	British &/or French & Other	177,990	4.1	British &/or French & Other	42,575	3.4
Other multiple origins	692,385	3.1	Other multiple origins	187,195	4.3	Other multiple origins	63,685	5.1

(1) Immigrants who came to Canada between 1981 and 1991.
(2) Includes the single responses of French, Acadian and Québécois.
(3) Includes the single responses of English, Irish, Scottish, Welsh and Other British, n.i.e..
(4) Includes the single responses of Inuit, Metis and North American Indian.
(5) Includes the single responses of Black, African Black, n.i.e. and Ghanaian.
(6) Includes persons who report more than one of the following origins: English, Irish, Scottish, Welsh and Other British, n.i.e..
(7) Includes persons who report more than one of the following origins: French, Acadian and Québécois.

n.i.e. = not included elsewhere.

Source: 1991 Census of Canada, unpublished data.

Regional Diversity

The ethnic make-up of Canada's population varied considerably across the country in 1991, in large measure reflecting where immigrants have settled over time. The Atlantic provinces had the highest proportion of people with British ancestry (62%), while Quebec had the highest proportion of those reporting French-only origins (75%). A number of non-British, non-French ethnic groups have also made Quebec their home. For example, the largest Arab and Haitian communities in Canada were in Quebec.

The attraction of Ontario for immigrants was reflected in the diversity of ethnic groups living in this province in 1991. About 40% of Ontario's population reported ethnic origins other than British or French. Some of Canada's largest ethnic communities were in Ontario. Over half of all persons reporting West Asian (54%), South Asian (55%), African (70%), Caribbean (63%) and Black (67%) single-ethnic origins lived in Ontario.

The Prairie provinces had Canada's highest proportions of persons reporting origins other than British or French (excluding the Territories). People of European ancestry accounted for the largest percentage of those with origins other than British (23%) – reflecting earlier waves of immigration from Western and Eastern Europe to this region.

British Columbia has been the focus of recent immigration to Canada from Asia; and this is reflected in the growing proportion of single Asian ethnic groups settling in this province. One out of nine British Columbia residents was of Asian origin in 1991. Although British Columbia had a higher proportion of persons of Asian origin than other provinces, Ontario had the largest number of persons reporting single Asian origins at 679,610, 7% of the province's population.

Linguistic Diversity in Canada

Immigration has also altered the linguistic profile of Canadian society. The percentage of the population who reported a language other than English or French as their mother tongue grew from 11% in 1986 to 13% in 1991,[5] largely due to the growth in the number of recent immigrants whose mother tongue is neither English or French. In 1991, 22% of persons who had a single mother tongue other than English or French had come to Canada in the past decade, compared with 18% prior to 1961. Much of the increase in non-official languages occurred in Ontario, British Columbia and Quebec, where most recent arrivals have settled.

---

[5]   Single responses for mother tongue and home language have been used in this study.

Overall, immigrants accounted for two-thirds of persons whose mother tongue was neither English nor French. In contrast, immigrants made up just 9% of persons with English as their single mother tongue and 2% of those with French as their single mother tongue.

The picture was similar for the languages Canadians speak most often at home. Immigrants were more likely to report a home language other than English or French: three out of four people speaking a non-official language at home were immigrants.

Table 2.4
Most Frequent Mother Tongues for the Canadian-born and Immigrants, Canada, 1991

Canadian-born

	Number	Percent
Total	22,427,745	100.0
Total single responses	22,214,790	99.1
English	14,643,705	65.3
French	6,360,660	28.4
Non-official language	1,210,420	5.4
1. German	210,205	0.9
2. Italian	171,630	0.8
3. Ukrainian	141,390	0.6
4. Chinese	83,925	0.4
5. Cree	73,750	0.3
Total multiple responses	212,955	0.9

Immigrated before 1961

	Number	Percent
Total	1,239,035	100.0
Total single responses	1,215,590	98.1
English	456,810	36.9
French	28,975	2.3
Non-official language	729,800	58.9
1. Italian	172,095	13.9
2. German	168,090	13.6
3. Dutch	87,860	7.1
4. Polish	44,655	3.6
5. Ukrainian	38,040	3.1
Total multiple responses	23,445	1.9

All immigrants

	Number	Percent
Total	4,342,890	100.0
Total single responses	4,232,595	97.5
English	1,473,120	33.9
French	135,570	3.1
Non-official language	2,623,900	60.4
1. Chinese	388,670	8.9
2. Italian	334,570	7.7
3. German	252,705	5.8
4. Portuguese	159,570	3.7
5. Polish	142,635	3.3
Total multiple responses	110,295	2.5

Recent immigrants (1)

	Number	Percent
Total	1,238,450	100.0
Total single responses	1,198,765	96.8
English	284,615	23.0
French	37,375	3.0
Non-official language	876,775	70.8
1. Chinese	220,195	17.8
2. Spanish	80,265	6.5
3. Polish	74,115	6.0
4. Arabic	52,615	4.2
5. Punjabi	47,610	3.8
Total multiple responses	39,685	3.2

(1) Immigrants who came to Canada between 1981 and 1991.

Source: 1991 Census of Canada, unpublished data.

Statistics Canada – Catalogue No. 96-311E
Canada's Changing Immigrant Population

The Language Profile of Recent Immigrants

Seventy-one percent of immigrants who came to Canada between 1981 and 1991 reported a mother tongue other than English or French, compared with 59% of those who came before 1961. Three of the five most frequently reported non-official languages for recent arrivals were non-European **(Table 2.4)**. In contrast, for those who came before 1961, all five of the largest non-official mother tongues were European. While Italian, German and Dutch were the most frequently reported non-official mother tongues among immigrants who arrived prior to 1961, those languages were not among the top five non-official mother tongues for recent immigrants.

The proportion of immigrants reporting French as their single mother tongue remained relatively stable regardless of the period of immigration. For example, 2% of those who came before 1961 reported French as their single mother tongue, compared with 3% of recent arrivals. On the other hand, the proportion of immigrants reporting English as their single mother tongue declined, from 37% of immigrants who came before 1961 to 23% of those who came between 1981 and 1991.

The picture was similar for the languages spoken most often at home. Among recent immigrants, the proportion of English as home language declined and conversely, the proportion of non-official home language increased. Recent immigrants were the most likely to report a non-official language as their home language (56%), compared with 35% of all immigrants and 2% of the Canadian-born population. The majority of immigrants (73%) who came before 1961 reported English only as the language most often spoken at home in 1991. This proportion declined to 33% for recent immigrants. The decline in the proportion of those speaking English at home by period of immigration was partly due to the increase of non-official language groups among recent immigrants and the increase of earlier immigrants speaking English at home.

On the other hand, the proportion of those speaking French at home has increased slightly by period of immigration, from 3% of immigrants who came before 1961 to 4% of recent arrivals. As well, the languages spoken at home by recent arrivals differed from earlier arrivals. Chinese and Polish were the top two non-official home languages among recent immigrants, followed by Spanish, Vietnamese and Punjabi. In comparison, among immigrants who came before 1961, the top five non-official home languages were all European.

Table 2.5
Most Frequent Home Languages for the Canadian-born and Immigrants, Canada, 1991

Canadian-born	Number	Percent		All immigrants	Number	Percent
Total	22,427,745	100.0		Total	4,342,890	100.0
Total single responses	22,197,490	99.0		Total single responses	4,098,520	94.4
English	15,711,005	70.1		English	2,423,835	55.8
French	6,033,250	26.9		French	168,885	3.9
Non-official language	453,235	2.0		Non-official language	1,505,800	34.7
1. German	51,520	0.2		1. Chinese	319,390	7.4
2. Cree	50,765	0.2		2. Italian	196,645	4.5
3. Chinese	47,200	0.2		3. Portuguese	106,310	2.4
4. Italian	41,335	0.2		4. Polish	90,520	2.1
5. Punjabi	24,230	0.1		5. Spanish	87,735	2.0
Total multiple responses	230,255	1.0		Total multiple responses	244,365	5.6

Immigrated before 1961	Number	Percent		Recent immigrants (1)	Number	Percent
Total	1,239,035	100.0		Total	1,238,450	100.0
Total single responses	1,194,410	96.4		Total single responses	1,147,510	92.7
English	904,600	73.0		English	406,985	32.9
French	31,735	2.6		French	51,430	4.2
Non-official language	258,075	20.8		Non-official language	689,095	55.6
1. Italian	100,075	8.1		1. Chinese	197,995	16.0
2. German	33,370	2.7		2. Polish	62,430	5.0
3. Ukrainian	19,105	1.5		3. Spanish	61,585	5.0
4. Polish	16,305	1.3		4. Vietnamese	41,885	3.4
5. Greek	13,225	1.1		5. Punjabi	40,435	3.3
Total multiple responses	44,615	3.6		Total multiple responses	90,930	7.3

(1) Immigrants who came to Canada between 1981 and 1991.

Source: 1991 Census of Canada, unpublished data.

Statistics Canada – Catalogue No. 96-311E
Canada's Changing Immigrant Population

Immigrants and Knowledge of the Official Languages

According to the 1991 Census, most immigrants had knowledge of Canada's official languages, with 79% of all immigrants reporting that they could conduct a conversation in English only, 4% in French only and 12% in both English and French. The remaining 6% (273,000) said that they were unable to conduct a conversation in either English or French. More than one-half (55%) of the latter group resided in Ontario, 18% were in British Columbia and 15% were in Quebec. About one-third of immigrants who spoke neither English or French reported Chinese as their mother tongue, another 16% reported Italian, 12% reported Portuguese and 5% reported Punjabi.

Recent immigrants made up the largest percentage of immigrants unable to converse in either of the official languages. In 1991, just over one-half of those who spoke neither English nor French came to Canada between 1981 and 1991. As indicated by **Chart 2.2**, the longer immigrants reside in Canada, the more likely they are to acquire a knowledge of at least one of the official languages.

Chart 2.2
**Immigrants by Knowledge of Official Languages and Period of Immigration,
Canada, 1991**

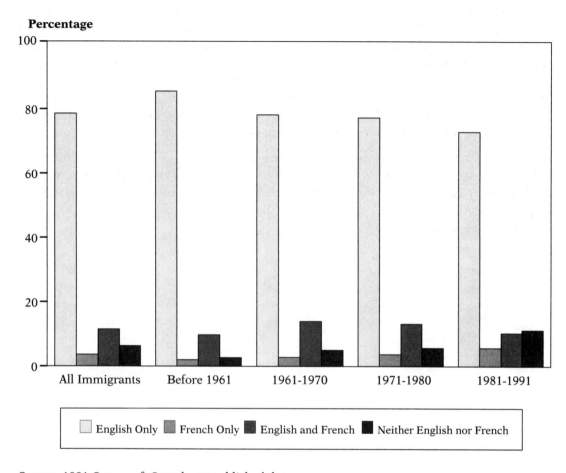

Source: 1991 Census of Canada, unpublished data.

Chapter

3

Demographic Characteristics of Canada's Immigrants

Various waves of immigration over the years have resulted in an immigrant population with a slightly different demographic profile than the Canadian-born population. These differences affect the overall demographic composition of Canadian society and the role of immigrants in the labour force.

Most Came as Young Adults

Most people immigrate to Canada as young adults. According to the 1991 Census, 37% of immigrants were aged 25 to 44 when they came to Canada. Another 27% arrived when they were aged 15 to 24, while 28% were younger than 15. On the other hand, 8% of all immigrants were 45 years and over when they immigrated to Canada. Overall, the median age of Canada's immigrant population at the time of immigration was 23.6 years.

The age at which people came to Canada as immigrants varied by place of birth. Immigrants born in the United States had the lowest median age at immigration (20.3 years), while those from Eastern Asia had the highest (27.2 years).

... But an Increasing Proportion Immigrated at Older Ages

Although nearly two-thirds (62%) of recent immigrants were aged 15 to 44 when they arrived, the proportion of older people immigrating to Canada has increased. For example, 15% of immigrants who came to Canada between 1981 and 1991 were 45 years or older when they arrived, compared with 2% of those who came before 1961. Of those who came before 1961, less than 1% were aged 65 years and over when they immigrated. In comparison, 3% of recent immigrants were in this age group when they came to Canada. This trend towards older immigrants is also reflected in the median age at immigration. For people who came to Canada before 1961, the median age at immigration was 21.1 years. This median age increased to 23.4 years for those who came during the 1960s, to 23.7 years for those who arrived in the 1970s, and to 26.7 years for those who came within the last decade.

The increase of older immigrants was more pronounced for women than for men: 16% of immigrant women who came in the last decade were 45 years or older, compared with 13% of men.

The trend of older persons immigrating to Canada is likely a reflection of Canada's immigration policy, which favours reunification of family members. This may have led to an increased number of older relatives such as parents joining their adult children in Canada.

An Older Immigrant Population

Since most immigrants came to Canada as young adults, the age structure of the immigrant population is markedly different from that of persons born in Canada. The immigrant population had both a higher proportion of older persons and a lower proportion of children than did the Canadian-born population. One reason this population is older is that children born after immigrants have settled in Canada are counted as Canadian-born rather than as part of the immigrant population.

In 1991, 5% of all immigrants, compared with 24% of the Canadian-born, were younger than 15. The situation was reversed at the other end of the scale with 18% of immigrants and 10% of those born in Canada aged 65 and over. In fact, one out of every four persons aged 65 and over in Canada was an immigrant. In contrast, 4% of the population younger than 15 were immigrants.

The contrast in age composition between immigrants and the Canadian-born is visible in the shape of their respective population pyramids (**Chart 3.1**). The age distribution of the immigrant population is represented by an inverted pyramid, indicating a relatively older population. In contrast, the Canadian-born population is represented by an upright pyramid, indicating a younger population.

Chart 3.1
Age-Sex Distribution of Immigrant and Canadian-born Populations, Canada, 1991

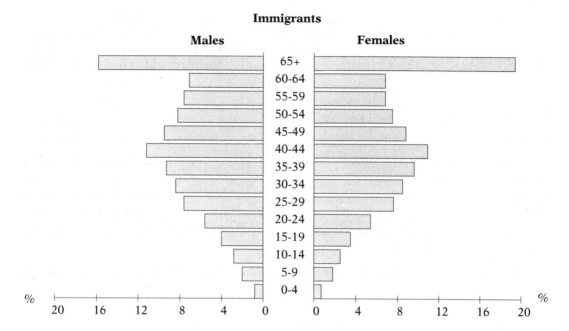

Source: 1991 Census of Canada, unpublished data.

Provincial Variations

The differences in the age profile of immigrants and those born in Canada is further reflected in the median age of these populations. In 1991, the median age for immigrants was 44.5 years, compared with 31.0 years for the Canadian-born. The age of immigrants, however, varied by province. Saskatchewan had the oldest immigrant population with a median age of 55 years, while the Northwest Territories had the youngest median age at 40.4 years. In the three provinces with the largest concentration of immigrants – Ontario, British Columbia and Quebec – the median age of immigrants was similar to the national figure. The median age of Ontario's immigrant population was 44.4 years, compared with 45.8 years in British Columbia and 43.4 years in Quebec.

Chart 3.2
Median Age of Immigrants and the Canadian-born, 1991

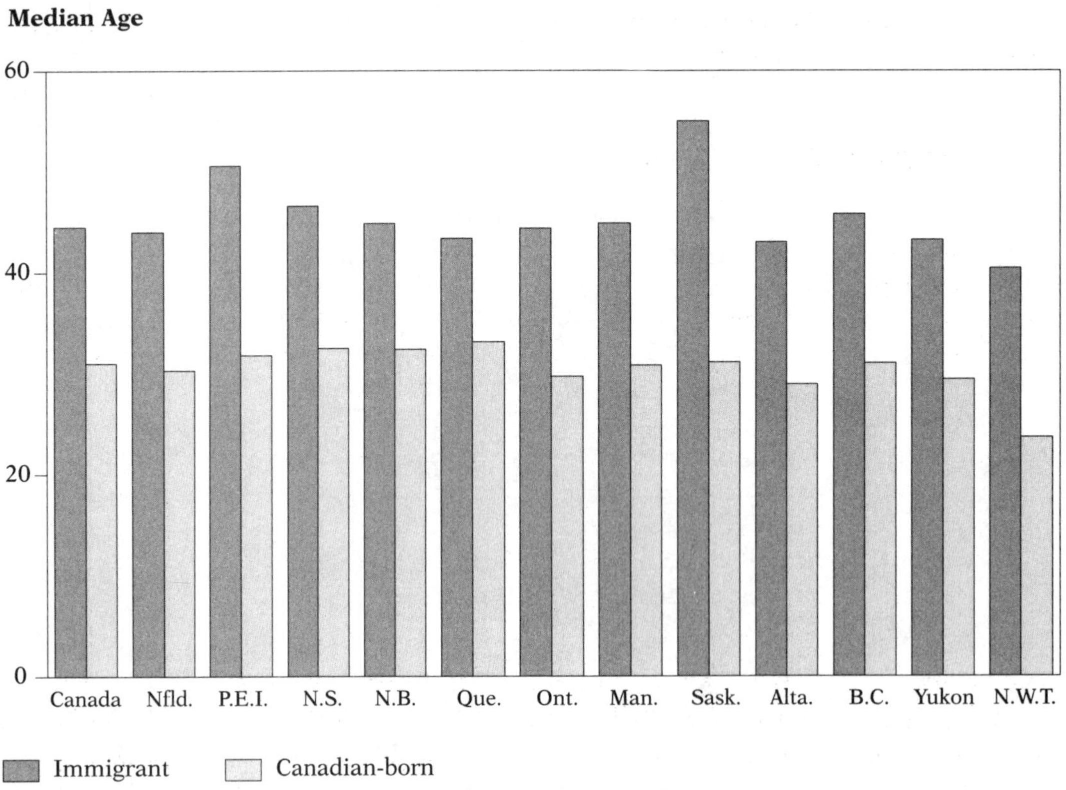

Median Age

■ Immigrant   ☐ Canadian-born

Source: 1991 Census of Canada, unpublished data.

Immigrant Population Reduced Canada's Dependency Ratio

One demographic consequence of a population's age composition is the number of economically dependent persons relative to its potentially active persons in the labour force. The "child dependency ratio" compares the number of people under 15 years of age to the number of people of working age (15 to 64 years). The "old-age dependency ratio" compares those aged 65 and over with the working age population. These two indices are expressed as the number of children and elderly per 100 population of those economically active.

Since relatively few immigrants came as children, the child dependency ratio for immigrants was low (6.9) compared with that of the Canadian-born (38.3). On the other hand, the old-age dependency ratio was higher for immigrants (22.9) than for the Canadian-born (14.5).

The higher proportion of immigrants in the working age groups also contributed to the reduction of Canada's overall dependency ratio. In 1991, the overall dependency ratio for immigrants was 29.8, while that for the Canadian-born was 52.9. The combined dependency ratio for Canada as a whole was 48.1. In other words, immigrants have a higher proportion of people of working age than do the Canadian-born.

More Immigrant Women Than Men

Historically, more men than women have immigrated to Canada. Over the decades, however, the gap in the ratio of males to females[1] has gradually narrowed, largely due to the increase of women immigrating to Canada and the higher survival rate of women. At the time of the 1981 Census, immigrant women outnumbered immigrant men for the first time. According to the 1991 Census, there were slightly fewer men than women among immigrants than in the Canadian-born population. For the immigrant population, there were 96.3 men per 100 women, compared with 97.9 men per 100 women for the Canadian-born. The ratio for recent immigrants was similar to that for the total immigrant population.

Variations by Sex and Place of Birth

The number of men and women coming to Canada is affected partly by demographic and socio-economic factors in the countries of origin and partly by Canada's immigration policy. According to the 1991 Census, there were considerable variations in the ratio of immigrant men to women by country of birth.

---

[1]   The sex ratio is the number of men per 100 women and is used to assess the relative number of men and women within a population.

The regions of birth with the highest ratio of men to women for all immigrants were: Western Asia and the Middle East (127.2), Africa (115.6) and Southern Europe (109.1). On the other hand, the ratio was lowest for the United States (76.1), the Caribbean (78.3) and the United Kingdom (86.1), indicating that more women than men immigrate from these regions. Similarly, there was a higher ratio of men to women among recent arrivals from Western Asia and the Middle East, Africa, Eastern Europe, Southern Europe and Southern Asia. The ratio was lowest for recent arrivals from the United States, the Caribbean and Oceania.

Table 3.1
Male/Female Ratio by Place of Birth for All Immigrants and Recent Immigrants (1), Canada, 1991

Place of birth	All immigrants	Recent immigrants
Total	**96.3**	**96.3**
U.S.A.	76.1	74.2
Central & South America	96.9	97.0
Caribbean & Bermuda	78.3	76.6
United Kingdom	86.1	89.4
Northern Europe	96.4	84.8
Western Europe	101.2	89.6
Eastern Europe	100.7	104.8
Southern Europe	109.1	104.4
Africa	115.6	123.9
Western Asia & the Middle East	127.2	129.1
Eastern Asia	93.6	92.5
South East Asia	89.4	86.1
Southern Asia	106.9	103.8
Oceania & Other	88.2	80.9

(1) Immigrants who came to Canada between 1981 and 1991.

Male/female ratio is the number of males per 100 females.

Source: 1991 Census of Canada, unpublished data.

Higher Proportion of Married Immigrants

At the time of the 1991 Census, immigrants were more likely to be married than were their Canadian-born counterparts. Of those aged 15 and over, 66% of immigrants were married, compared with 52% of the Canadian-born. The proportion of persons widowed was also higher for immigrants: 8% compared with 5% of people born in Canada. At the same time, immigrants were less likely to be single. One-third of Canadian-born persons aged 15 and over had never married, compared with just 18% of immigrants.

These differences in marital status partly reflect the different age structure of the immigrant population compared with the Canadian-born. The proportion of older persons was higher among immigrants, hence they were more likely to be married. The data also suggest that the Canadian-born delay marriage longer than do immigrants: the proportion of married was higher for immigrants than for the Canadian-born, in all age groups **(Table 3.2)**. For example, among those aged 15 to 24, 7% of the Canadian-born and 12% of immigrants were married. The proportion of married immigrants aged 25 to 44 was 71%, whereas the corresponding figure for the Canadian-born was 60%.

Table 3.2
Percentage Distribution of Marital Status by Age for the Canadian-born and Immigrants, Canada, 1991

Marital status	Total (1) Cdn-born	Immigrant	Age 15 to 24 Cdn-born	Immigrant	Age 25 to 44 Cdn-born	Immigrant	Age 45 to 64 Cdn-born	Immigrant	Age 65+ Cdn-born	Immigrant
Total	100.0	100.0	100.0	100.0	100.0	100.0	100.0	100.0	100.0	100.0
Single (2)	33.5	18.4	92.4	86.8	28.2	19.5	7.5	4.7	7.8	4.1
Married (3)	51.9	66.2	6.8	12.0	59.8	71.3	72.9	80.4	56.7	59.0
Separated	2.8	2.7	0.5	0.6	3.7	3.4	3.7	3.1	1.9	1.8
Divorced	6.3	4.9	0.3	0.4	7.7	5.2	10.2	6.8	3.3	3.3
Widowed	5.4	7.8	0.0	0.1	0.5	0.5	5.7	5.0	30.3	31.9

(1) Population 15 years and over.
(2) Never married persons.
(3) Includes married and common-law union.

Source: 1991 Census of Canada, unpublished data.

Fertility

Immigrant women had slightly more children than did women born in Canada. Overall, in 1991, the average number of children ever born to immigrant women aged 15 to 44, either currently or previously married was 1,816 per 1,000, compared with 1,738 for Canadian-born women. As well, in 1991 83% of ever-married immigrant women aged 15 to 44 had borne at least one child, compared with 81% of Canadian-born women.

However, the number of children born to immigrant women varied by place of birth. Immigrant women born in Central America had the highest average number of children (2,341 per 1,000). They were followed by immigrant women from Western Asia and the Middle East (2,043) and Southern Europe (2,023). Immigrant women from Eastern Europe (1,533), Eastern Asia (1,573) and Oceania (1,703) had the lowest average number of children.

Chart 3.3
Children Ever Born Per 1,000 Ever-married Immigrant and Canadian-born Women Aged 15 to 44 by Place of Birth, 1991

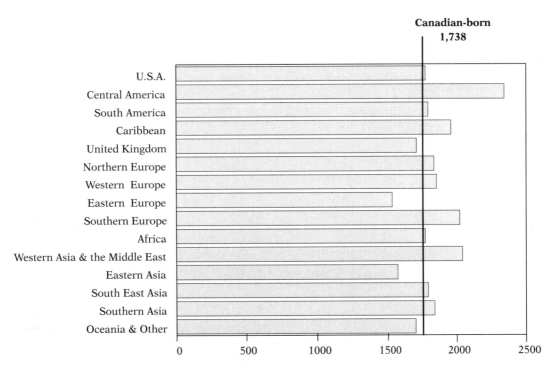

Source: 1991 Census of Canada, unpublished data.

Chapter

4

Educational Attainment of Immigrants

The 1991 Census showed that a higher proportion of immigrants had university degrees than did the Canadian-born. At the same time, however, a larger percentage of immigrants than the Canadian-born reported less than Grade 9 education.

Relatively High Proportion With University Education ...

Immigrants were more likely to have higher levels of education than the Canadian-born. About 14% of immigrants aged 15 and over had university degrees, compared with 11% of the Canadian-born. The difference was evident for both men and women. Among immigrant men, 17% had a university degree, compared with 12% of men born in Canada. As for immigrant women, 12% held university degrees, as opposed to 9% of their Canadian-born counterparts. The higher level of educational attainment of Canada's immigrants is partly due to Canada's immigration policy since the 1960s, which has tended to emphasize educational achievement and occupational qualifications in selecting immigrants.

... But Also a Higher Proportion With Less Than Grade 9 Education

At the same time, a higher proportion of immigrants (19%) than the Canadian-born (13%) had less than Grade 9 education. Immigrant women were more likely than immigrant men to have less than Grade 9 schooling: 21% of immigrant women reported this educational level, compared with 16% of immigrant men and 13% of Canadian-born women.

As with the Canadian-born, immigrants with less than Grade 9 education were more likely to be older. In 1991, 40% of immigrants and 39% of persons born in Canada with less than Grade 9 were aged 65 and over. Many of these people completed their formal schooling at a time when educational opportunities and expectations were quite different from today.

Chart 4.1
Highest Level of Education for the Canadian-born and Immigrants Aged 15 Years and Over, Canada, 1991

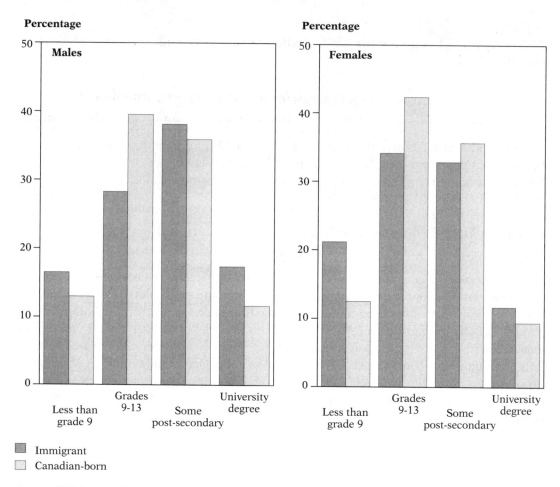

Source: 1991 Census of Canada, unpublished data.

Regional Variations in Educational Level of Immigrants

The overall median years of schooling for immigrants was 12.8 years, with slight variations across the provinces. Immigrants in the Northwest Territories (14.6 years) and Newfoundland (14.5 years) had the highest median years of schooling, while immigrants residing in Saskatchewan and Manitoba had the lowest median years (each at 12.2 years). The latter partly reflects the settlement in these provinces of earlier immigrants with less formal education. In contrast, among the Canadian-born, those living in Ontario had the highest median years of schooling (12.6 years), whereas those residing in the Northwest Territories (10.9 years) and Newfoundland (11.4 years) had the lowest.

Table 4.1
Median Years of Schooling for the Canadian-born and Immigrants Aged 15 Years and Over, 1991

	Canadian-born			Immigrant		
	Total	**Male**	**Female**	**Total**	**Male**	**Female**
Canada	**12.5**	**12.4**	**12.5**	**12.8**	**13.1**	**12.6**
Newfoundland	11.4	11.3	11.4	14.5	15.0	13.9
Prince Edward Island	12.1	11.6	12.4	13.0	13.3	12.9
Nova Scotia	12.1	12.0	12.2	13.8	14.7	13.2
New Brunswick	12.1	12.0	12.2	13.0	13.6	12.8
Quebec	12.2	12.2	12.2	12.7	13.2	12.2
Ontario	12.7	12.7	12.7	12.8	13.1	12.7
Manitoba	12.2	12.1	12.2	12.2	12.4	12.0
Saskatchewan	12.2	12.1	12.4	12.2	12.3	12.1
Alberta	12.6	12.6	12.6	12.8	13.0	12.6
British Columbia	12.6	12.6	12.6	12.9	13.2	12.7
Yukon Territory	12.6	12.5	12.7	13.9	14.1	13.6
Northwest Territories	10.9	10.9	10.8	14.6	14.8	14.4

Source: 1991 Census of Canada, unpublished data.

Educational Profile of Recent Immigrants

The larger proportion of university degree holders among the total immigrant population is partly a result of the higher educational levels of recent arrivals. Overall, 17% of immigrants who came between 1981 and 1991 had a university degree, compared with 9% of immigrants who arrived before 1961. The difference was more pronounced for those aged 25 and over: 21% of recent immigrants had a university education, compared with 9% of immigrants who came before 1961.

Both male and female recent immigrants tended to have higher levels of education than those who came in earlier years. In 1991, 25% of immigrant men aged 25 and over who came in the last 10 years held a university degree, as opposed to 19% of all immigrant men and 12%

of those who arrived before 1961. As for immigrant women, 17% of recent arrivals had completed university, compared with 12% of all immigrant women and 6% of those who arrived before 1961.

Although recent immigrants tended to have higher levels of education, a number of them, especially among the older age groups, had less than Grade 9 schooling. In 1991, 14% of recent immigrants did not have a Grade 9 education. Among recent arrivals aged 65 and over, almost half (47%) had less than a Grade 9 education. In this age group, one-half of immigrant women had less than Grade 9 education, compared with just over one-third (38%) of immigrant men.

Chart 4.2
Highest Level of Education for Immigrants Aged 15 Years and Over, Showing Selected Periods of Immigration, Canada, 1991

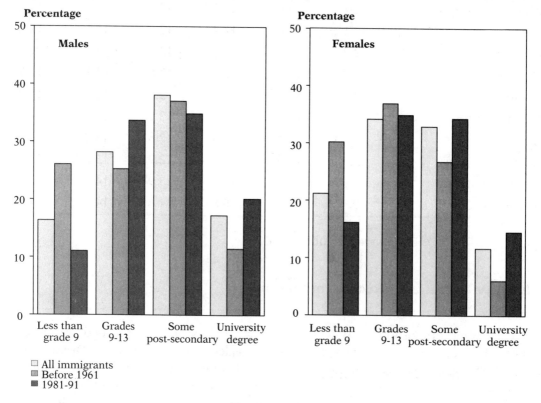

Source: 1991 Census of Canada, unpublished data.

Variations by Place of Birth

Educational levels varied considerably among immigrants from different regions. Immigrants from the United States, Africa and Asia had the highest proportions of persons with university degrees, ranging from 22% to 28%. Immigrants from Southern Europe and Central America had the lowest proportions, at 4% and 8%.

Immigrants from Southern Europe (48%), Eastern Europe (25%) and Central America (24%) had the highest proportions with less than Grade 9, while immigrants from Africa had the lowest proportion (6%), followed by those from the United Kingdom (7%), the United States and the Caribbean (9% each).

Table 4.2
Highest Level of Education by Place of Birth for Immigrants Aged 15 Years and Over, Canada, 1991

Place of birth	Total		Less than grade 9	Grades 9-13	Some post-secondary	University degree
	Number		Percent			
Total	**4,112,070**	**100.0**	**18.9**	**31.2**	**35.5**	**14.4**
U.S.A.	231,415	100.0	8.9	28.3	34.6	28.2
Central America	53,475	100.0	23.9	34.3	33.7	8.0
South America	138,520	100.0	10.0	37.6	41.4	10.9
Caribbean & Bermuda	218,645	100.0	8.9	36.1	45.4	9.6
United Kingdom	702,435	100.0	6.8	38.7	42.1	12.4
Northern Europe	81,310	100.0	15.1	29.9	43.7	11.4
Western Europe	421,960	100.0	12.3	27.2	48.5	12.0
Eastern Europe	398,415	100.0	25.4	26.3	34.5	13.7
Southern Europe	699,020	100.0	47.6	26.8	21.3	4.3
Africa	153,525	100.0	6.2	27.3	41.1	25.5
Western Asia & the Middle East	125,240	100.0	13.1	32.3	32.6	22.0
Eastern Asia	346,140	100.0	17.4	31.1	29.0	22.5
South East Asia	280,435	100.0	15.1	32.5	34.0	18.4
Southern Asia	217,690	100.0	13.9	32.4	29.1	24.6
Oceania & Other	43,840	100.0	9.5	33.3	41.9	15.3

Source: 1991 Census of Canada, unpublished data.

Immigrants and School Attendance

Overall a lower proportion of immigrants (14%) than the Canadian-born (19%) was attending school. However, in each age group, a higher proportion of immigrants than the Canadian-born was attending school in all age groups. This was because of the large proportion of immigrants over the age of 45. Almost one-half (49%) of the immigrant population were 45 years of age and over, compared with just over one-quarter (27%) of the Canadian-born.

In general, immigrants were more likely to attend school part-time and less likely to attend full-time than the Canadian-born. About 57% of immigrants who were attending school, attended full-time, as opposed to 69% of the Canadian-born. On the other hand, 43% of immigrants, compared with 31% of the Canadian-born, attended school part-time.

Chapter

5

Immigrants In The Labour Force

At various stages in Canada's history, immigrants have been admitted to meet the demand for specific kinds of labour in the Canadian economy. This process, together with changes in the source countries and demographic characteristics of recent immigrants, have influenced both the educational and labour force characteristics of the immigrant population. This chapter explores the labour force profile of Canada's immigrants.

Labour Force Participation of Immigrants

In 1991, the overall labour force participation rate[1] of immigrants was 65.2%, slightly higher than in 1986 (64.7%). However, this 1991 rate for immigrants was lower than that for the Canadian-born (68.7%). As well, differences in rates were greater for women than men in 1991. The participation rate of immigrant women was 56.5%, compared with 60.8% of Canadian-born women. As for immigrant men, 74.3% were in the labour force, compared with 77.0% of Canadian-born men. Participation of immigrants in the labour force, however, varied considerably by age, length of residence in Canada, educational attainment and knowledge of English or French.

Age and Labour Force Participation

Since participation in the labour force is in part related to age, any comparison of labour force rates for the immigrant and Canadian-born populations is affected by their different age structures. In general, younger immigrants tended to have lower labour force participation rates than their Canadian-born counterparts, while immigrants in older age groups had higher rates. For example, among men aged 15 to 24, 65.5% of immigrants and 69.7% of the Canadian-born were in the labour force. Likewise, the participation rate of women in the same age group was higher for those born in Canada than for immigrants: 65.5% compared with 62.6%. The lower labour force participation rate for these immigrants

---

[1] The labour force participation rate is the percentage of the population 15 years of age and over (excluding institutional residents) who were in the labour force (employed or unemployed) during the week prior to Census Day (the reference week).

may be partly attributed to the fact that more immigrants than the Canadian-born in this age group were attending school.

Among those aged 25 to 44, both male and female immigrants had similar participation rates to those of their Canadian-born counterparts **(Table 5.1)**. However, for persons aged 45 years and older, immigrants were more likely than the Canadian-born to be in the labour force. For example, among those aged 45 to 64, 84.1% of immigrant men were in the labour force, compared with 79.2% of Canadian-born men. Similarly, immigrant women in this age group had a higher participation rate than their Canadian-born counterparts, 60.1% compared with 56.2%.

Table 5.1
Labour Force Participation Rate by Age Group, Sex and Period of Immigration, for the Canadian-born and Immigrants, Canada, 1991

	Canadian-born	All immigrants	Period of immigration			
			Before 1961	1961-70	1971-80	1981-91
Population aged 15+						
Total	**68.7**	**65.2**	45.1	75.8	76.9	69.2
Male	77.0	74.3	55.5	85.3	84.7	77.8
Female	60.8	56.5	35.2	66.6	69.4	61.2
Aged 15 to 24						
Total	**67.6**	**64.0**	n.a.	86.9	70.1	56.3
Male	69.7	65.5	n.a.	88.1	70.7	58.3
Female	65.5	62.6	n.a.	85.6	69.6	54.2
Aged 25 to 44						
Total	**86.9**	**86.1**	89.9	88.5	88.2	82.1
Male	94.6	93.8	96.2	95.4	95.5	90.7
Female	79.3	78.8	83.3	81.9	81.4	73.7
Aged 45 to 64						
Total	**67.5**	**72.3**	66.2	78.9	79.9	64.1
Male	79.2	84.1	79.1	89.4	90.0	77.9
Female	56.2	60.1	52.4	68.1	68.9	51.8
Aged 65+						
Total	**9.3**	**9.7**	9.3	10.4	9.1	12.5
Male	14.3	14.6	13.7	16.2	14.7	19.8
Female	5.6	5.9	5.7	6.3	5.6	7.4

n.a.= not applicable
Source: 1991 Census of Canada, unpublished data.

Length of Residence in Canada and Labour Force Participation

The labour force activity of immigrants also varied according to the length of time they had been in Canada **(Table 5.1)**. The labour force participation rate of recent immigrants (69.2%) was lower than for immigrants who arrived in the 1960s (75.8%) and 1970s (76.9%). Recent immigrants may take time to adapt to Canada's labour market and to acquire language skills in either English or French. Hence they are less likely to participate fully in the labour force than those who have been in the country for some time. The lowest labour force participation rate, however, was among those who came before 1961 (45.1%). Most of these immigrants were in the older age groups: 70% were 55 years of age and over, and were therefore less likely to be in the labour force.

Recent immigrants had lower labour force participation rates than those who arrived earlier, in all age groups, except age 65 and over. The labour force participation rate of recent immigrant men aged 45 to 64 was 77.9% compared with 89.4% of men who arrived in the 1960s and 90.0% of those who arrived in the 1970s. For immigrant women, the rate was 51.8% for recent arrivals, as opposed to 68.1% and 68.9% of those who came to Canada in the 1960s and 1970s, respectively.

The largest difference in participation rates was among those aged 15 to 24. However, comparison between earlier immigrants and recent arrivals in this age group needs to take into account that those who immigrated between 1961 and 1970 would be 22 to 24 years of age in 1991, and therefore were more likely to participate in the labour force.

Variations by Place of Birth

Labour force participation rates for immigrants also varied considerably by birthplace. Immigrant men from Africa, Southern Asia, the Caribbean, Central and South America and Oceania had the highest rates, ranging from 84.3% to 80.4%. On the other hand, men born in Eastern Europe had the lowest participation rate (57.3%).

Among those who came within the past decade, immigrant men from European countries generally had higher labour force participation rates, with those from Northern Europe having the highest (88.6%). As well, recent arrivals from Africa and Southern Asia had participation rates of over 80%. The lowest rate for recent men was among immigrants from Eastern Asia (68.3%).

Participation rates for all immigrant women varied more than those for men, ranging from 72.3% for women from the Caribbean to 41.1% for women from Eastern Europe. Among recent immigrant women, the highest participation rates were observed for those from Northern Europe, Eastern Europe, South East Asian and Western Europe. The lowest rates were for recent immigrant women born in Western Asia and the Middle East and Eastern Asia.

Table 5.2
Labour Force Participation Rate by Place of Birth, Sex and Selected Periods of Immigration, for Immigrants Aged 15 Years and Over, Canada, 1991

	All immigrants		Immigrated before 1961		Recent immigrants (1)	
	Male	Female	Male	Female	Male	Female
Total	**74.3**	**56.5**	**55.5**	**35.2**	**77.8**	**61.2**
U.S.A.	72.0	55.1	43.0	24.8	79.1	61.9
Central & South America	82.4	65.8	77.4	56.7	78.4	59.9
Caribbean & Bermuda	83.6	72.3	66.0	54.6	76.8	65.6
United Kingdom	70.1	51.5	49.2	32.1	82.7	63.8
Northern Europe	66.6	51.6	51.7	36.8	88.6	70.8
Western Europe	75.9	54.8	69.0	45.7	84.7	65.8
Eastern Europe	57.3	41.1	38.6	22.2	82.6	67.3
Southern Europe	75.8	53.1	62.2	40.5	85.0	58.2
Africa	84.3	67.5	72.9	51.3	82.8	63.2
Western Asia & the Middle East	77.4	51.9	71.7	41.0	75.3	49.7
Eastern Asia	73.6	57.9	68.5	41.8	68.3	54.1
South East Asia	78.8	70.1	60.4	41.4	75.0	66.4
Southern Asia	84.2	65.1	62.0	43.7	81.7	60.8
Oceania & other	80.4	65.0	58.9	40.4	78.9	61.9

(1) Immigrants who came to Canada between 1981 and 1991.

Source: 1991 Census of Canada, unpublished data.

Educational Attainment and Labour Force Participation

Higher levels of schooling generally increase people's opportunities to participate in the labour market. Among immigrant men, labour force participation rates were lowest for those with less than Grade 9 schooling (52.3%), but highest for those with a university degree (87.8%). Similarly, immigrant women's participation in the labour force increased with higher levels of education, from 30.4% for those with less than Grade 9 education to 80.2% for those with a university degree.

Immigrants with less than Grade 9 schooling were more likely than the Canadian-born to participate in the labour force. For example, 89.1% of immigrant men aged 25 to 44 with less than Grade 9 education were in the labour force, compared with 77.8% of their Canadian-born counterparts. The difference in participation rate between immigrant and Canadian-born women in this age group was more pronounced: 65.5% compared with 47.4% of Canadian-born women.

On the other hand, immigrants with a university degree had a lower labour force participation rate than the Canadian-born with the same educational background. Among men with a university degree, 87.8% of immigrants, compared with 90.2% of the Canadian-born, were in the labour force. This trend was similar for women: 80.2% of immigrant women were in the labour force, compared with 84.7% of the Canadian-born.

Participation rates for the university-educated, however varied according to age. While younger university-educated immigrants had lower labour force participation rates than their Canadian-born counterparts, older immigrants with a university education had slightly higher rates. For example, among men aged 25 to 44 with university degrees, 95.3% of immigrants and 97.2% of the Canadian-born were in the labour force. Likewise, university-educated immigrant women in this age group had a lower participation rate than Canadian-born women: 85.3% compared with 90%. On the other hand, immigrants aged 45 to 64 had higher participation rates than persons born in Canada. For example, among women in this age group, 81.2% of immigrants with a university degree were in the labour force, compared with 79.7% of the Canadian-born. Among men, 91.4% of immigrants and 90.1% of the Canadian-born were in the labour force.

Table 5.3
Labour Force Participation Rate by Age Group, Sex and Highest Level of Education for the Canadian-born and Immigrants Aged 15 Years and Over, Canada, 1991

	Less than grade 9		Grades 9-13		Some post-secondary		University degree	
	Male	Female	Male	Female	Male	Female	Male	Female
Total								
Canadian-born	46.9	21.6	73.2	54.6	87.7	75.6	90.2	84.7
Immigrant	52.3	30.4	68.8	50.9	81.7	70.6	87.8	80.2
Aged 15 to 24								
Canadian-born	47.0	30.1	60.3	51.6	88.8	86.0	89.5	90.1
Immigrant	63.2	48.0	54.9	49.8	80.0	77.6	81.7	81.1
Aged 25 to 44								
Canadian-born	77.8	47.4	93.5	72.8	96.4	84.4	97.2	90.0
Immigrant	89.1	65.5	92.0	74.0	94.8	82.4	95.3	85.3
Aged 45 to 64								
Canadian-born	65.0	31.8	79.6	54.7	84.8	69.2	90.1	79.7
Immigrant	74.6	42.7	81.6	57.1	87.2	71.7	91.4	81.2
Aged 65+								
Canadian-born	10.5	3.4	14.5	5.6	16.8	8.4	28.6	13.4
Immigrant	9.7	3.7	13.0	5.7	17.8	9.7	29.6	16.2

Source: 1991 Census of Canada, unpublished data.

Knowledge of the Official Languages and Labour Force Participation

Immigrants' participation in the labour force is often associated with their knowledge of Canada's official languages. In general, immigrants who could not converse in English or French were the least likely to participate in the labour force. In fact, just 28.5% of immigrant women who were unable to converse in English or French were in the labour force. On the other hand, immigrants who knew both English and French had the highest labour force participation rate among the immigrant population. The labour force participation rate was 80.8% for immigrant men who could converse in both English and French, and 67.9% for immigrant women. In comparison, the labour force participation rate for Canadian-born men who could converse in English and French was 79.4%; it was 67.7% for Canadian-born women.

Chart 5.1
Labour Force Participation Rate by Sex and Knowledge of Official Languages for Immigrants Aged 15 Years and Over, Canada, 1991

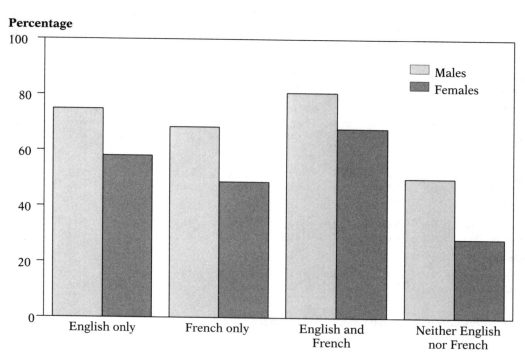

Source: 1991 Census of Canada, unpublished data.

Immigrants and Work Activity

Persons who were employed in 1990 can be divided into those working full-time and those working part-time.[2] Immigrant men and women were more likely than their Canadian-born counterparts to work full-time. Among men, 92% of immigrants worked full-time, compared with 89% of the Canadian-born. Proportionately more immigrant women worked full-time (77%) than did the Canadian-born (72%). In general, women – Canadian-born and immigrant – were more likely than men to work part-time: 23% of immigrant women and 28% of Canadian-born women compared to 8% of immigrant men and 11% of Canadian-born men.

---

[2] In 1991, full-time work referred to persons working full weeks (30 hours or more per week) in 1990. Part-time work referred to persons working less than 30 hours per week.

Chapter

6

Immigrants and Their Occupations

The 1991 Census showed that the occupations[1] of immigrants differed from the Canadian-born population, and that among immigrants, occupations varied by place of birth.

The Picture for Immigrant Men

Immigrant men were more likely than Canadian-born men to be employed in professional (17%), managerial and administrative (15%), service (11%), product fabricating (10%) and processing occupations (8%) **(Chart 6.1)**. These five occupational groups accounted for nearly two-thirds (62%) of all immigrant men in the experienced labour force, compared with just over one-half (52%) of Canadian-born men. On the other hand, comparatively fewer immigrant men worked in construction trades (10%) or primary (3%), sales (8%), and other (10%) occupations.

Among immigrant men who came to Canada within the last decade, nearly one-third were employed in either professional or service occupations. Relatively high proportions of recent arrivals were also employed in product fabricating (12%) and managerial and administrative occupations (11%). Recent immigrant men were least likely to work in primary occupations (3%).

---

[1]   The figures used in this chapter pertain to "the experienced labour force". As defined for the 1991 Census, this refers to persons who, during the week prior to June 4, 1991, were employed or unemployed but who had worked since January 1, 1990.

Chart 6.1
Percentage Distribution of Major Occupation Group for Canadian-born and Immigrant Men Aged 15 Years and Over, Canada, 1991

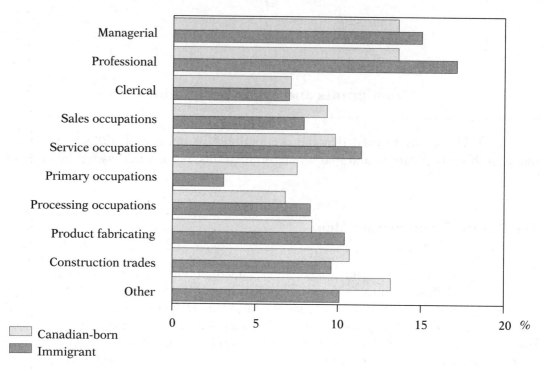

Source: 1991 Census of Canada, unpublished data.

The occupational characteristics of immigrants also varied by birthplace, especially for recent immigrants. In 1991, nearly one-third of recent immigrant men from the United States were employed in professional jobs. Relatively high proportions of recent arrivals from the United Kingdom (25%), Northern Europe (27%), Western Europe (20%), Africa (21%) and Eastern Asia (20%) were also employed in these occupations. Recent immigrant men from Central America (20%), Eastern Asia (22%), South East Asia (20%) and Oceania (19%) were more likely to be employed in service occupations. As well, almost one-third of recent immigrant men from Southern Europe worked in construction occupations, while men born in South East Asia (18%), South America (16%) and the Caribbean (15%) had the highest concentrations in product fabricating jobs.

Table 6.1
Major Occupation Group by Place of Birth for Recent Immigrant Men (1), Canada, 1991

Place of birth	Total Number	Total Total	Managerial admin. & related	Professional & related	Clerical & related	Sales	Service	Primary	Processing	Product fabricating	Construction trades	Other
							Percent					
Total	**407,160**	**100.0**	**10.5**	**15.4**	**8.8**	**7.8**	**16.2**	**2.7**	**8.5**	**11.5**	**7.8**	**10.8**
U.S.A.	12,905	100.0	17.3	30.8	6.9	8.5	9.0	4.6	3.1	4.9	7.0	7.7
Central America	15,950	100.0	4.6	8.7	7.9	3.4	20.3	6.6	11.9	13.9	9.7	12.9
South America	22,140	100.0	7.8	11.2	11.8	5.8	16.1	0.9	10.2	15.7	7.7	12.8
Caribbean & Bermuda	21,670	100.0	6.5	9.0	12.9	6.5	17.5	1.2	10.8	15.0	6.3	14.5
United Kingdom	23,670	100.0	16.6	25.2	6.4	8.6	9.1	3.4	5.8	9.4	7.1	8.3
Northern Europe	3,035	100.0	14.0	26.5	5.4	7.9	7.6	3.0	6.8	9.9	12.5	6.8
Western Europe	13,780	100.0	19.4	20.4	4.2	6.7	10.7	12.5	6.7	7.5	5.8	6.1
Eastern Europe	44,720	100.0	4.8	17.2	4.8	4.9	11.6	2.2	12.3	14.2	15.3	12.7
Southern Europe	22,480	100.0	4.5	7.3	3.8	4.1	14.0	3.7	9.9	10.4	32.5	10.0
Africa	29,050	100.0	13.2	20.6	13.4	9.8	16.4	0.8	5.1	7.6	2.7	10.5
Western Asia & the Middle East	34,630	100.0	13.0	15.4	10.6	12.1	16.5	0.9	4.8	10.9	5.6	10.3
Eastern Asia	62,150	100.0	17.7	19.6	9.2	12.3	21.7	1.0	4.0	5.8	2.8	6.0
South East Asia	54,390	100.0	5.2	10.0	9.3	5.8	19.5	1.9	13.2	18.0	4.7	12.3
Southern Asia	42,640	100.0	9.4	10.3	10.6	6.8	15.2	4.6	10.7	11.6	4.9	15.8
Oceania & Other	3,945	100.0	8.1	14.1	8.4	8.4	19.4	2.4	6.7	15.3	7.2	10.0

(1) Immigrants who came to Canada between 1981 and 1991.

Source: 1991 Census of Canada, unpublished data.

The Picture for Immigrant Women

Immigrant women were more likely than Canadian-born women to be employed in service (17%), processing (3%) and product fabricating (8%) occupations. In fact, immigrant women were proportionately four times more likely than their Canadian-born counterparts (2%) to work in product fabricating jobs. As with Canadian-born women, about one-half of immigrant women were concentrated in clerical (28%) and professional (20%) occupations, although fewer immigrant women than the Canadian-born worked in these occupations.

Chart 6.2
Percentage Distribution of Major Occupation Groups for Canadian-born and Immigrant Women Aged 15 Years and Over, Canada, 1991

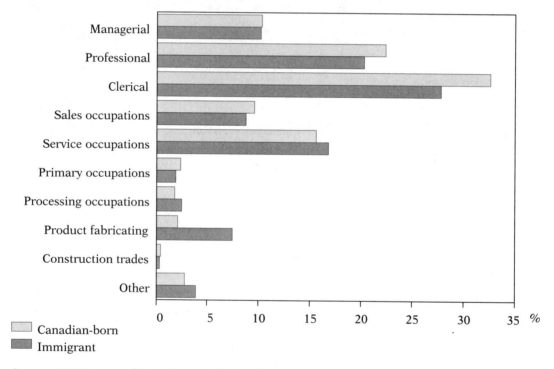

Source: 1991 Census of Canada, unpublished data.

Female recent immigrants were more concentrated in service (22%), processing (3%) and product fabricating (10%) occupations than all immigrant women and the Canadian-born. On the other hand, the proportion of female recent immigrants in professional (17%) and clerical occupations (26%) was lower than that of all immigrant women and the Canadian-born.

The occupational characteristics of recent immigrant women also varied by birthplace. As with men, recent immigrant women born in the United States were most likely to work in professional occupations (32%). These occupations also contained high concentrations of women from the United Kingdom (24%), Northern Europe (27%), and Western and Eastern Europe (each at 24%). While there were high proportions of women from all regions in clerical occupations, those from Africa (36%), the United Kingdom (32%), Eastern Asia (31%) and Western Asia and the Middle East, South America, Northern Europe and Caribbean (each at 30%), were most likely to be employed in these jobs. The highest proportions of recent immigrant women in service occupations were born in Southern Europe (31%) and Central America (30%), while recent arrivals from Southern Europe and South East Asia (each at 16%) and Central America (15%) had the highest concentration in product fabricating occupations.

Table 6.2
Major Occupation Group by Place of Birth for Recent Immigrant Women (1), Canada, 1991

Place of birth	Total Number	Total	Managerial admin. & related	Professional & related	Clerical & related	Sales	Service	Primary	Processing	Product fabricating	Construction trades	Other
							Percent					
Total	**350,795**	**100.0**	**6.7**	**17.2**	**26.0**	**8.3**	**21.7**	**2.0**	**3.1**	**9.6**	**0.3**	**5.1**
U.S.A.	16,935	100.0	12.6	32.1	24.5	9.7	14.5	2.7	0.9	0.9	0.2	1.9
Central America	11,435	100.0	3.5	12.5	17.6	5.1	29.9	5.6	3.6	15.0	0.7	6.4
South America	20,080	100.0	6.0	13.4	30.1	7.6	19.8	0.5	2.7	12.0	0.4	7.4
Caribbean & Bermuda	26,135	100.0	4.6	18.1	29.7	7.6	22.9	0.2	3.0	8.1	0.2	5.6
United Kingdom	22,165	100.0	10.4	23.5	32.2	10.9	16.3	1.9	0.6	2.0	0.2	2.0
Northern Europe	3,225	100.0	10.7	26.7	29.8	11.2	17.1	0.6	0.5	0.8	0.5	1.9
Western Europe	13,060	100.0	12.3	24.4	22.9	10.4	16.9	7.3	1.5	2.1	0.3	1.7
Eastern Europe	35,590	100.0	4.0	24.1	17.7	8.0	25.8	1.0	4.3	8.3	0.7	6.2
Southern Europe	15,610	100.0	3.7	9.1	16.1	6.5	31.1	2.0	6.8	16.4	0.7	7.7
Africa	18,295	100.0	8.7	19.6	35.6	9.1	17.2	0.3	1.7	4.3	0.2	3.3
Western Asia & the Middle East	17,040	100.0	7.8	17.8	30.4	14.1	17.7	0.4	1.7	7.3	0.2	2.6
Eastern Asia	57,245	100.0	9.4	13.9	30.5	9.8	19.6	0.6	2.6	10.3	0.2	3.2
South East Asia	58,910	100.0	4.1	14.3	22.3	5.2	26.8	1.2	4.2	15.7	0.3	6.0
Southern Asia	30,865	100.0	4.8	9.4	25.7	7.1	17.5	8.1	4.6	12.1	0.4	10.4
Oceania & Other	4,220	100.0	5.1	19.2	28.4	9.1	27.5	1.7	1.4	3.0	0.0	4.5

(1) Immigrants who came to Canada between 1981 and 1991.

Source: 1991 Census of Canada, unpublished data.

Statistics Canada – Catalogue No. 96-311E
Canada's Changing Immigrant Population

Where Immigrants Worked: Major Industry Groups

In 1991, the largest proportion of all immigrant men was employed in manufacturing industries (23%). The next largest concentration was trade industries (16%), followed by service (13%) and finance, insurance and real estates industries (12%). In contrast, 18% of Canadian-born men worked in manufacturing industries, 17% in the trade sector, and 9% each in service and finance, insurance and real estate industries. As well, immigrant men had proportionally lower concentrations in primary and government service industries than men born in Canada. Almost one in ten Canadian-born men was employed in primary industries, compared with less than one in twenty immigrant men. About 9% of Canadian-born men were in government service industries, compared with 5% of immigrant men.

Immigrant women, on the other hand, were most likely to be employed in service industries (17%), followed by trade and health and social service industries (each at 16%). In comparison, women born in Canada had the highest concentrations in trade (18%), health and social service as well as other service industries (each at 16%). The largest differences in concentration between immigrant and Canadian-born women were in manufacturing and government services industries. Immigrant women were more likely than Canadian-born women to be employed in manufacturing industries: 15% compared with 9%. As for government service industries, Canadian-born women had a higher concentration than immigrant women: 8% compared with 5%.

Chart 6.3
Percentage Distribution of Major Industry Group for the Canadian-born and Immigrants Aged 15 Years and Over, Canada, 1991

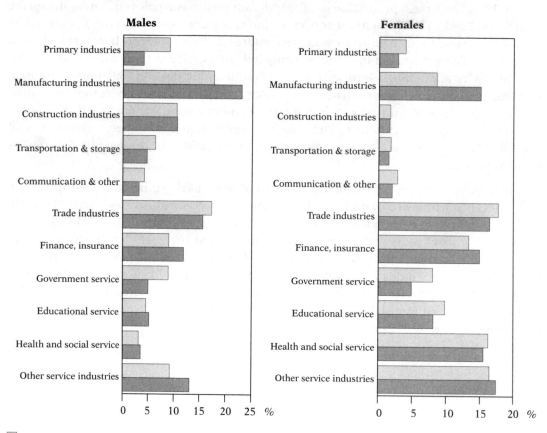

☐ Canadian-born

■ Immigrant

Source: 1991 Census of Canada, unpublished data.

Chapter

7

Non-permanent Residents

For the first time in 1991, the Census enumerated non-permanent residents in addition to immigrants. Non-permanent residents are persons who at the time of the Census, held student or employment authorizations, Minister's permits or who were refugee claimants. This chapter profiles this segment of the population.

Where They Live

The Census counted 223,410 non-permanent residents residing in Canada in 1991. This was slightly less than 1% of the total population. Over half (56%) of all non-permanent residents enumerated in the Census lived in Ontario. Quebec had the next largest proportion (20%), followed by British Columbia (13%) and Alberta (6%). The other provinces and territories accounted for 5%.

As with the immigrant population, most non-permanent residents lived in Canada's three largest metropolitan areas, with Toronto having the largest concentration. In 1991, 44% of Canada's non-permanent residents lived in Toronto, 18% in Montreal and 10% in Vancouver.

As a result of this concentration, non-permanent residents represented a notable proportion of the population of these urban centres. Although they accounted for 0.8% of the national population, non-permanent residents made up 2.5% of the population in Toronto, 1.3% in Montreal and 1.4% in Vancouver. Windsor had the next highest proportion, at 0.9%. In other major metropolitan areas, non-permanent residents made up less than 1% of the population.

Table 7.1
Non-permanent Residents, Canada, Provinces, Territories and Selected CMAs, 1991

	Total population	Non-permanent residents	% Total population
Canada	**26,994,045**	223,410	0.8
Newfoundland	563,940	835	0.1
Prince Edward Island	128,100	125	0.1
Nova Scotia	890,950	1,700	0.2
New Brunswick	716,495	1,355	0.2
Quebec	6,810,300	43,970	0.6
Ontario	9,977,055	126,165	1.3
Manitoba	1,079,390	4,025	0.4
Saskatchewan	976,040	2,875	0.3
Alberta	2,519,185	14,085	0.6
British Columbia	3,247,505	28,035	0.9
Yukon Territory	27,660	90	0.3
Northwest Territories	57,430	155	0.3
Selected Census Metropolitan Areas			
Toronto	3,863,110	98,105	2.5
Vancouver	1,584,120	22,345	1.4
Montreal	3,091,115	40,050	1.3
Windsor	259,290	2,220	0.9
Ottawa-Hull	912,095	7,285	0.8
Hamilton	593,805	4,500	0.8
Kitchener	353,110	2,680	0.8

Source: Statistics Canada, *Immigration and Citizenship*. 1991 Census of Canada, Catalogue No. 93-316.

Where They Came From

The largest proportion of non-permanent residents (44%) was born in Asia and the Middle East. Others were from Europe (19%), Central and South America (11%), Africa (9%), the United States (8%), the Caribbean (7%) and Oceania (2%).

The major countries of birth for non-permanent residents differed from those of recent immigrants. The United States was the most frequent source country for non-permanent residents, followed by the Philippines and Sri Lanka. In contrast, Hong Kong was the major country of birth of landed immigrants who came to Canada within the last decade, followed by Poland and China. Overall, the top ten places of birth accounted for 47% of non-permanent residents in Canada.

Table 7.2
Top 10 Places of Birth for Non-permanent Residents and Recent Immigrants (1), Canada, 1991

	Non-permanent residents			Recent immigrants	
	Number	**%**		**Number**	**%**
Total	**223,410**	**100.0**	**Total**	**1,238,455**	**100.0**
1. United States	18,155	8.1	1. Hong Kong	96,540	7.8
2. Philippines	15,095	6.8	2. Poland	77,455	6.2
3. Sri Lanka	12,655	5.7	3. People's Republic		
4. Hong Kong	10,950	4.9	of China	75,840	6.1
5. People's Republic			4. India	73,105	5.9
of China	10,945	4.9	5. United Kingdom	71,365	5.8
6. United Kingdom	9,300	4.2	6. Viet Nam	69,520	5.6
7. Iran	8,185	3.7	7. Philippines	64,290	5.2
8. Trinidad & Tobago	7,035	3.1	8. United States	55,415	4.5
9. Japan	6,830	3.1	9. Portugal	35,440	2.9
10. India	5,755	2.3	10. Lebanon	34,060	2.7

(1) Immigrants who came to Canada between 1981 and 1991.

Source: 1991 Census of Canada, unpublished data.

More Women Than Men

There were slightly more women than men (100 to 99) among the non-permanent residents enumerated in the Census. The proportion of male to female non-permanent residents, however, varied by country of birth. There was a higher proportion of men than women among non-permanent residents born in Western Asia and the Middle East, Africa and Southern Asia. The ratios of men to women from these regions ranged from 145 to 184. On the other hand, more women than men came from Northern Europe, the United Kingdom and South East Asia, with the ratios ranging from 73 to 30.

Young Population with Few Seniors

The non-permanent resident population enumerated in the 1991 Census was relatively young. The proportion of non-permanent residents younger than 15 was almost three times that of the total immigrant population: 14% versus 5%. Compared with recent immigrants, non-permanent residents had a lower proportion of persons younger than 15, but a higher proportion of those aged 15 to 24 (22%). About one-half of non-permanent residents (51%) were aged 25 to 44. This is a higher proportion than for all immigrants (37%) and for recent immigrants (48%).

On the other hand, the proportion of older persons among non-permanent residents was much smaller than that for the immigrant population. About 9% of non-permanent residents were aged 45 and 64, compared with 31% of all immigrants and 13% of recent arrivals. Just 4% of non-permanent residents were aged 65 and over, compared with 18% of all immigrants and 6% of those who came between 1981 and 1991.

Another measure of the age structure of a population is median age. The median age was 28.6 years for non-permanent residents, lower than both the Canadian-born population (31.0) and the immigrant population (44.5).

Marital Status

The younger age structure of the non-permanent resident population was reflected in its marital status characteristics. Compared with immigrants, non-permanent residents were more often single. Among those aged 15 and over, 45% of non-permanent residents had never married, compared with just 18% of all immigrants and 30% of recent immigrants. Only 46% of non-permanent residents were married, compared with 66% of all immigrants and 60% of recent arrivals.

Knowledge of the Official Languages

Three out of four non-permanent residents, a slightly lower proportion than immigrants, reported they were able to conduct a conversation in English only. On the other hand, a higher proportion of non-permanent residents could converse in French only: 5% compared with 4% of all immigrants. About 10% of non-permanent residents, compared with 12% of all immigrants, could conduct a conversation in both English and French. One in nine non-permanent residents was unable to conduct a conversation in either of Canada's official languages. This level was similar for landed immigrants who came within the last decade (11%), but higher than for the total immigrant population (6%).

Highly Educated

Non-permanent residents had higher levels of schooling than the immigrant population – a reflection in part of the foreign student component of this group. About 20% of non-permanent residents aged 15 and over had a university degree in 1991. This compares with 14% of all immigrants and 17% of recent immigrants. In fact, one-third of all non-permanent residents reported having some university education, with or without a degree. On the other hand, just 11% of non-permanent residents aged 15 and over, had less than Grade 9 schooling, compared with 19% of all immigrants and 14% of recent immigrants.

Chart 7.1
Highest Level of Education for all Immigrants, Recent Immigrants (1) and Non-permanent Residents, Canada, 1991

Percentage

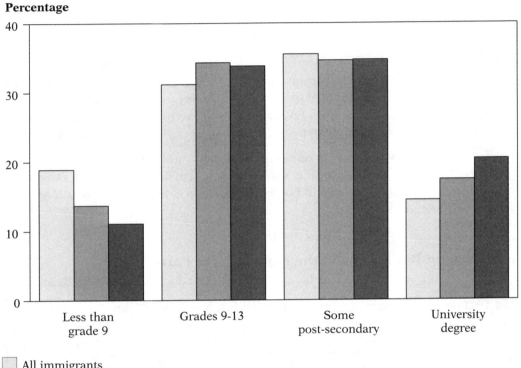

□ All immigrants
▨ Recent immigrants
■ Non-permanent residents

(1) Immigrants who came to Canada between 1981 and 1991.

Source: 1991 Census of Canada, unpublished data.

Another measure of educational attainment is median years of schooling. Non-permanent residents generally had higher median years of schooling than immigrants. For those aged 25 and over, the median years of schooling was 13.7 years for non-permanent residents, compared with 12.8 years for all immigrants and 13.5 years for recent immigrants. Men in the non-permanent resident population had higher levels of schooling than did women: 14.0 years for men compared with 13.4 years for women.

The educational attainment of non-permanent residents varied by province. Non-permanent residents in Newfoundland (16.8 years), Saskatchewan (16.5 years) and Nova Scotia (16.2 years) had the highest median years of schooling. The two provinces with the highest concentration of non-permanent residents, Quebec (13.4 years) and Ontario (13.6 years), along with New Brunswick (13.2 years), had the lowest median years of schooling. Nevertheless, non-permanent residents even in these provinces generally had higher median years of schooling than immigrants.

Foreign Students

Foreign students accounted for just over one-third (35%) of all non-permanent residents aged 15 and over enumerated in the Census. Most foreign students (65%) studied full-time. Nearly one-third were from Eastern Asia, followed by 12% from Africa and 9% from Western Asia and the Middle East.

More male foreign students than female were studying full-time: 55% compared with 45%. Conversely, 64% of all part-time students were female. The largest number of part-time foreign students were born in South East Asia (26%), Central and South America (12%) and Southern Asia (11%).

Non-permanent Residents and the Labour Force Participation

In 1991, six out of every ten non-permanent residents aged 15 and over were in the labour force. Non-permanent residents, however, had lower participation rates than immigrants: 59.7% compared with 65.2% for all immigrants and 69.2% for recent immigrants. Labour force participation rates for non-permanent residents peaked at 71.2% for those aged 25 to 44. The lower rate for non-permanent residents may reflect the high foreign student component among this group, as well as the fact that refugee claimants are not able to work until they are given an employment authorization by Canadian immigration authorities.

Among non-permanent residents, women had a lower rate of participation in the labour force (53.5%) than men (66%). Labour force participation rates for both men and women peaked for those aged 25 to 44, at 77.2% and 65.1%.

Participation in the labour force for non-permanent residents also varied by level of educational attainment. Overall, increased educational attainment was associated with higher labour force participation, with university degree holders having the highest rate -- 75.4% for men and 60.5% for women. The exception was for women with a university education and some postsecondary education: labour force participation rates were the same for both levels of education. Labour force participation rates for non-permanent residents with less than Grade 9 education were 61.5% for men and 33.5% for women.

Conclusion

Data from the 1991 Census show that Canada's immigrant population is changing. Although immigrants' share of the total population has remained relatively stable over the years, their cultural and socio-demographic characteristics have changed considerably.

Recent immigrants who came to Canada between 1981 and 1991 were mostly attracted to British Columbia, Ontario, Quebec and Alberta, especially to the urban areas of these provinces. They were more likely to have been born in non-European countries, especially Asia, the Middle East, the Caribbean and, Central and South America. This change in immigrants' place of birth has altered the ethnic and linguistic composition of Canada. Recent immigrants were more likely to report ethnic backgrounds other than British or French and languages other than English or French. While most came as young adults, an increasing proportion also arrived at older ages.

In general, recent immigrants were more likely to have a university degree than were all immigrants and the Canadian-born population. At the same time, a number of recent arrivals, especially among the older age groups, had less than Grade 9 schooling. The participation rate in the labour force of recent immigrants was lower than that of immigrants who came in the 1960s and 1970s. Recent arrivals may take time to adapt to Canada's labour market and to acquire the official languages, hence are less likely to participate fully in the labour force. Labour force participation rate increased for those who have been in the country for some time. While immigrants were employed in all occupational and industrial groups, they were concentrated in certain occupations and industries, such as professional, managerial, service and product fabricating occupations for immigrant men, and clerical, professional, service and product fabricating occupations for immigrant women. The occupational characteristics of immigrants also varied by place of birth.

All in all, immigrants comprised an important segment of Canada's population and economy, and have played a major role in creating a socio-cultural mosaic.